ENGLISH
HOME STYLE

ENGLISH
HOME STYLE

Pam Boys

ARCH CAPE PRESS

CLB 2271
© 1990 Colour Library Books Ltd., Godalming, Surrey, England.
© Illustrations: Michael Boys Syndication, England..
This 1990 edition published by Arch Cape Press,
a division of dilithium Press, Ltd.
distributed by Crown Publishers, Inc.
225 Park Avenue South, New York, New York 10003.
Printed and bound in Hong Kong.
All rights reserved.
ISBN 0 517 68211 7
h g f e d c b a

CONTENTS

INTRODUCTION

This book is not intended as a digestion of style, but as a visual commentary on the diverse frameworks in which we can live. It traces the pattern of living, from the early part of this century to the Eighties, within forty differing English homes.

The approach to creating a background for life is a reflection of the individual's personality, and through it an interesting form of decorative motivation emerges. The fundamental reason may arise out of creative expression, the wish to provide a social background, sensitivity to heritage, passion for space, or the more practical requirements for solo or family living.

The trends are set by the professional who perfects the art of architectural design and decoration and the assembling of exquisite objects to create a particular design, by the practical designer who has perfected the skill through experience, or by those who have a constant need to change style, either in their existing home or perhaps even in a succession of homes. Interest in historical correctness governs others, who get satisfaction in the re-creation of an era. Some have an intuitive sense of colour and texture in making their environment. And there are those who create style as a release for inventive energy and for the joy of living.

The diversity of homes featured ranges from a small mews house to manor houses and a castle. Conversions of derelict garages, stables, a greenhouse in the sky and a triumphal arch all illustrate the undaunted energy of some owners in creating a home.

The ever increasing interest in interiors and commercial influences for change turn the whole question of how people live into an intriguing subject. Style is not necessarily linked to extravagance, it is not always the smart and fashionable, but may be appreciation of light, form and colour combined with natural flair.

MORLEY OLD HALL
– A SIXTEENTH-CENTURY MOATED MANOR HOUSE

❖

Morley Old Hall lies in a quiet backwater of Norfolk. Found as a dignified ruin some years ago, the new owner was not intimidated by the enormity of the task ahead of her. Her own sense of scale and colour, allied to a desire for unpretentious comfort, has created a home with the character of the original house.

Houses which escape the changing fashions of the centuries have individual authority and, as such, command respect from their owners. When Janet Shand Kydd found Morley Old Hall, in the middle of East Anglia, the imposing wreck dominated the surrounding fields with the air of a 400-year-old patriarch. Yet the first joys of ownership were soon buffeted by advice from friends as to how to tackle the mammoth task of restoration. The house was too large for easy management, and the temptation was there to remove a wing or two, or reverse the house. Mrs Shand Kydd's own instinct – reinforced by David Mlinaric's advice – was to leave well alone.

Set in thirty acres of untended grounds grown luxurious with undisturbed wild flowers, the Hall is enclosed in just a quarter of an acre of garden surrounded by an Anglo-Saxon moat, which was probably dug seven hundred years ago to make the walls for an earlier dwelling. The half-mile-long driveway to the house used

Rose Kiftsgate cascades over the moat walls and heads of Lilium regale (above) stand out against the Dutch-gabled front elevation of Morley Old Hall.

Above: the full grandeur of the Hall seen at a distance through a sea of hemlock and wild flowers which flourish in the surrounding grounds.

to be rutted and hazardous for visitors as it wound through chestnut trees and daffodils but, once through the moat gate, the lovingly laid stone slabs were found to form inviting curves towards the entrance hall. Although the manor house presents an imposing facade with symmetrical cross wings on either side, its size is deceptive as it is only one room deep.

The only structural alterations made during renovation involved the removal of two walls in the main hall, one in order to gain a view of the stairs, and another in the entry hall. The owner immediately found that the original builders had erected these seemingly useless walls to stop the draughts, and so the builders were instructed to leave the rest of the structure well alone. All the materials for the restoration were searched out from old buildings – old bricks for the kitchen worktops and slate slabs for the floor came from a tumbled-down barn. Pammnents (square floor tiles from the neighbouring county of Suffolk) were found to cover the floor of the main hall – polished, they reflect a mellow amber and red glow from their well-worn surfaces.

The beams throughout the building have been limed to achieve an even, elderly grey, and the wall surfaces between them washed with a faded blush shade – the nearest colour to that of untreated plaster. The Hall has

Below: soft apricot walls and neutral furnishings in the entrance hall blend with the warm tones of the polished pamment floor. The view through to the staircase was gained by the removal of one draught excluding wall. The heat loss has been remedied by a large wood-burning stove set in the 'McBean Original' fireplace constructed from panels of Elizabethan woodwork.

Above: light slants in from windows on both sides of the Great Chamber on the first floor, with views down the drive and border garden.

Contrast in styles for two bedroom designs. The attic bedroom (above) is left free of any hangings, the four-poster bed set central in the 'triangular' shape. The only other furniture is a pair of chrome chairs and a glass tank filled with giant hemlock. The other distinct English country house bedroom (right) is furnished in faded rose tones, with Victorian needlepoint rugs and antique quilts. Chintz from Colefax and Fowler is used for the overlong curtains.

lost the darkening effect of Elizabethan oak panelling, as this was stripped and sold by a previous owner, so the overall effect of pink-washed walls and lightened beams gives a continuous feeling through the house, without the punctuations of sharp decorative changes.

The main entrance hall is low and inviting, having a wide, open fireplace. As the first one had decayed, the late Angus McBean was commissioned to create a 'McBean' original from panels of Elizabethan wood as a surround to the stone and brick fire. A long sofa covered in brown striped fabric is piled high with a mixture of brown and beige cushions. The only other furniture in the long, narrow room is an oversize fender stool covered in leather and a curved chest standing beneath the main window. A modern log-burning stove was necessary to counteract the draughts caused by the removal of the wall.

The Great Chamber on the intermediate floor of the hall was designed for the squire and his family to retire to for their entertainment, away from the area open to all-comers below. With light now filling the room from both sides, and an ample supply of comfortable sofas, it makes a lovely room for summer evenings, having views down the drive and border garden.

The two cross wings would have once been the parlour rooms for the family at the upper end, and the lower wing

the buttery, pantry and kitchen. One was changed to a 'Doggie Room' designed for people and large canine friends to relax in. Mrs Shand Kydd asked Angus McBean to decorate the room with pineapples. This he did by painstakingly measuring every conceivable space between the beam panels, doorways and windows, and then printing hessian with pineapples, foliage and arches, individually designed to fit each space. The designs in dull brick tones, mingled with blue, blend with the narrow Tudor bricks of the large open fire. That was the only statement needed to decorate the room. There are no curtains and just one portrait, of a lady with an Elizabethan ruff framing her face, a large sofa, and some tables lit by orange-shaded lamps.

The kitchen is planned as the hub of entertaining life at the Hall. Here are large vessels for the preparation of food for a crowd, rather than for formal dinner parties, one large dresser, a vast scrubbed table, open storage spaces built under brickwork surfaces and a refreshing lack of fitted cupboards. The room is filled with the smell of good cooking, mixed with the scent of drying herbs and the contents of vast bowls of pot pourri gathered from the garden.

In fact, simplicity is really the theme which runs through all Mrs Shand Kydd's decoration. The stairs

Left: antique lace for the hangings on the mahogany four-poster bed are an unusual combination with the country style patchwork quilt. Low lighting from four table lamps increases the warm tones of the apricot in the room.

could have been turned into an impressive feature in such a large hall, but they have been left as a simple ascent with a walnut tallboy at the foot. Paintings are hung so that they pick out the soft tones of the surrounding furnishings, and one is hardly aware of curtains, if they are used at all.

Mrs Shand Kydd does use curtains and drapes for the bedrooms. The main bedroom has rose chintz curtains from Colefax and Fowler made over-full and long to spread over the rose design needlepoint carpet, while

Above: the joys of country life are epitomised in the kitchen, where drying herbs and flower heads, vast wooden bowls with pot pourri gathered from the scented garden, chestnuts and home-baked bread make for a room designed for relaxed entertainment.

deep-winged leather armchairs and a day bed covered in an antique quilt bring comfort with style. A bamboo-framed cheval mirror reflects the painting of a pensive lady in a dark blue flowered hat. Another room has a Regency four-poster bed hung in antique cream lace, with a patchwork quilt of mostly brown, cream and grey squares, while a warmer apricot wash for the walls and warm shaded lights complement the mahogany furniture.

Way up in the loft space of the Hall, a four-poster bed set centrally under the pitch of the roof is left bare of any hangings, having simply a white antique crocheted counterpane to cover it. Hemlock from the fields placed in a glass tank on the floor makes a graphic arrangement here alongside the outline of two modern chrome and cane chairs.

The two bathrooms share the same lattice wallpaper, but different colours make dissimilar rooms. The brown version, with a vast white bath set in ochre-painted panels, has the windows softened with silk blinds, and welcomes one with a warm enclosed feel, while the larger bathroom, based on clear blue, has an antique silvered bath recessed in a giant marble slab. The mullioned windows go full height to the ceiling, and uncurtained, cast a cool light into the room, providing a great sense of space.

Creating a garden is as much an art as making a home, and Mrs Shand Kydd has achieved both at Morley Old Hall. The open courtyard has carefully laid stone slabs invitingly curved in fan shapes towards the arched door. All the roses at the front of the house are white and fall in great showers of blossom, half hiding the garden seats strategically placed for an appreciation of the view across the moat to the wild gardens beyond. The retaining brick walls of the moat are now covered in a profusion of Rose Kiftsgate, while in the moat itself Muscovy ducks and Brent geese enjoy the sheltered water.

The gardens to the rear of the Hall are designed as two borders with irregular edges, and the plants have been allowed to grow in a wild tangle of shrub roses, lilies, poppies and foxgloves mixed with ground cover plants. These cushion the flat facade of the extremely tall Dutch gabled elevation. Built for communal living, Old Morley Hall is essentially a family home. Her own children grown-up, Mrs Shand Kydd has now left the house, but she has ensured that it will bear her creative mark for years to come.

Left: solid pine tables and a tall dresser dominate the room with a refreshing lack of fitted cupboards. The tall mullioned windows are left bare of blinds or curtains. Trailing stems of a spider plant, silver candlesticks and a bronze head (above), making a quixotic hat stand, decorate the window ledges.

Above: a detail of the massed seed heads drying in readiness for vast arrangements to decorate the Hall.

A REVERSAL OF PERIODS AT ELSFIELD MANOR

Elsfield Manor has the genteel exterior one expects of an eighteenth-century building, but an explosive twentieth-century interior by Michael Haynes. Set in Oxfordshire, the house was once Sir John Buchan's home and a literary gathering place in the Thirties, and it is this period that underlies the owner's creations in perspex and plastic. Throughout, Haynes utilises the architectural background of the house simply as neutral cubic spaces for his original designs.

The classic, stone Elsfield Manor house was built in the eighteenth century. A less attractive brick and stone wing was a later addition, but the whole presents a traditional English country exterior. The three clay figures peering into a window give a hint of the electric shock waiting inside.

From its creeper-clad exterior set in the Oxfordshire countryside, Elsfield Manor appears to be an English country gentleman's traditional home. Once through the doors, however, a shock awaits. Personal living for Haynes is approached in much the same way as designing an exhibition. In his working life, Michael Haynes creates eye-stopping window displays and museum exhibitions in plastic, and his home is a *tour de force* along the same lines. When he purchased the eighteenth-century Manor, it had had no distinctive personality imposed upon it by its previous owners, yet it maintained the air of a well-appreciated home. Delving into the past, Haynes found that Sir John Buchan had lived there, writing all his novels in the library and holding house parties for his friends from London and

Left: in the library, the past is enlivened with perspex furniture designed by Michael Haynes. The dining room (above) is designed within a macramé tent hung from the ceiling. Light strikes shafts on the perspex table and chairs.

Oxford. This Thirties background and his own considerable enthusiasm for perspex gave Haynes the launching pad he needed to create an extraordinary home.

He was first drawn to perspex when he saw a box of off-cuts in sunlight and was fascinated by its ability to trap light. When he is not designing for exhibitions and is free from commercial strictures, he can make perspex look like a million dollars – though few can afford his prices for one-off pieces of handmade furniture. Certainly, transparent plastic takes on a new dimension through his eyes. Geometric designs painted on multiple sheets of clear plastic, set one behind the other, re-align to give faceted designs from different angles. He uses clear perspex that traps the light like a cube of ice for tables and chairs, and wraps coloured sheets of it round wooden frames for large sofas.

Michael Haynes' approach to creating the interior of Elsfield Manor was similar to an exhibition operation; he did not have an overall style for the house, but instead thought of individual designs within separate cubic spaces, meticulously planning these over a period of three years. As the reaction of light on plastic is the springboard for his designs, the natural lighting in certain rooms suggested the tone of colour and mood of the decor.

The sitting room, suffused with a gentle light from the creeper-framed windows, seemed right for a peachy Thirties mood with some Art-Deco angularity. This period is evoked in the superb perspex sofa, which is made from sheets of peach perspex on a wooden frame and upholstered in quilted satin. Grey, peach and cream satin cushions, quilted, embroidered and gathered, add to the opulence, while embroidered ivy leaves hang from the peach velvet curtains on either side of a geometric wall design by Haynes. The base of the square coffee table is made of perspex rods stacked log-cabin style, and a very tall chair, made of clear perspex in a lattice pattern, stands before the elegantly shuttered windows.

Facing page: a night effect has been created in the bedroom, where shaded navy and grey satin covers the perspex four-poster bed, and internally lit angular tables act as light boxes.

Right: the bathroom epitomises the effect of colour and light of a box of off-cuts which first drew Michael Haynes to design in perspex.

Above: detail of the geometric design 'painted' by multiple sheets of perspex to give a 3-D effect from different angles. A multi-facetted ceramic tea set stands on the circular table with a stacked ring base. The sitting room (right) centres round an angular Art Deco sofa to a Haynes design in peach satin cushioned in shaded and appliquéd quilted satins and lit by a branched Art Deco fitting. A tall perspex chair stands alongside an eighteenth-century ceramic figurine.

The volume of light in the dining room triggered the design for a room hung with macramé. Light from the large sash windows filters through the rope-coloured hangings which cover the walls and form a tented ceiling. Triangular, narrow-headed chairs glisten in the light round a rectangular table with box legs, so dining at Elsfield in the Eighties is like eating in a Bedouin tent of macramé at an ice-cold table of perspex. By comparison, the library, with its academic association and vistas across Otmoor, has been treated almost traditionally, though spiced with Haynes furniture.

On the dark side of the house, the rooms have been designed to give a night-light effect. Choosing deep electric blue, Michael Haynes designed his own four-poster bed of indigo perspex and hung it in deep blue velvet. The quilted cover is made in 'shaded' navy and grey satin in a box pattern. Angular tables in bright perspex are lit internally to give the effect of light boxes, while the back wall is almost entirely covered by a three-dimensional painting of layered plastic.

The bathroom is painted dark blue with panels of primary coloured perspex covering one whole wall in three-dimensional relief. Layers of perspex are also fixed as design panels on doors, throwing prism effects of mixed light into the room when the door is opened.

Lighting is from multi-branched chandeliers, diffused wall lights, light tables, the occasional table lamp and angular branched candle holders – all designed by Michael Haynes in the material which dominates his thoughts.

This extraordinary home comes from a designer who thinks experience is the best teacher. With no formal art training, Haynes progressed from creating window displays for Jaeger in the Sixties and providing the Mecca betting shops with a new image with turf green painted windows, to the fashion exhibition 'Through the Decades' at the Victoria and Albert Museum in London, and many more. He passionately believes in the rebirth of crafts in England and has a group of craftsmen under his wing; subsidising the rents for their work space gives him the opportunity to foster the best talents from the countless applicants.

Their work forms part of the decoration in his home. Clay heads by Jill Crowley on a marble fireplace in the sitting room are grouped with a tapestry design of a figure reading a newspaper by Joanna Buxton. His own furniture design is upholstered in blue satin with an iris design by Jill Parry, who also hand painted a translucent screen in the sitting room. Haynes also designed a special perspex showcase to display ceramic pieces by Alison Britton, Carol McNicoll and pots by Jacqueline Poncelet. Elsfield Manor bursts with creative design and craftsmanship, but though Michael Haynes enthuses a lot about the achievements of others, he is modest about his own.

Right: another view of the sitting room, and a hand-painted translucent screen of irises painted by Jill Parry, who also designed the quilted blue chair fabric. Michael Haynes designed the perspex showcase to display his collection of ceramic pieces by Alison Britton and Carol McNicoll and pots by Jacqueline Poncelet.

TRIUMPHAL ARCH IN NORFOLK

Designed in 1734 for the Earl of Leicester, this magnificent archway was intended merely as an ornamental edifice on the driveway to Holkham Hall over one mile away. Undaunted by the practical difficulties of entirely separate units, limited stair access and little interior space – or the additional handicap of the absence of water and electricity – architect Nicholas Hill has turned the structure into a whimsical 'home in the sky'.

The north Norfolk coast is seldom seen by tourists visiting England as East Anglia does not provide a throughway to other counties; most visitors to England will have seen Nelson's Column in Trafalgar Square, but few will have found his birthplace hidden down a narrow Norfolk lane. Being so far off the beaten track, the area has managed to withstand a lot of twentieth-century development pressures and much of it, particularly the coastal stretches, are National Trust property, or designated as areas of outstanding natural beauty. It was on a visit to Holkham Hall that Nicholas Hill and his family first saw the Triumphal Arch. Being an architect, Nicholas Hill was intrigued with the grandeur of the structure and became fired with the possibility of turning it into a weekend retreat. He wrote to the owners, enquiring if he could lease the property. Though it was a quixotic request, it met with a response. Enquiries were made of this stranger and eventually a lease was signed, and thus Nicholas Hill acquired what he describes as 'an eighteenth-century version of a tree house'.

The Arch was started in 1734 and, from records of accounts paid, was probably finished in 1761. Although

Facing page: seen by night, the structure presents a facsimile of the original sketches.

Above: bricks fired on the estate were 'rusticated' with stones gathered from fields and shore.

Above: bird's-eye view of the double-height dining room, showing the octagonal table and herringbone pattern of the old brick floor. Another view (left) of the same room shows the gallery added by Nicholas Hill to provide space for a dressing and shower bathroom above the kitchen. Right: a corner desk in the living room, with a much valued folio of Brettingham's engravings open at his plans for the building of the Triumphal Arch.

the land of the estate had been secured by the family just after the Elizabethan era, the house was not built until the eighteenth century. The Earl of Leicester, with his designer William Kent, would sketch facades of the final exterior they desired, handing the structure and depth planning over to Matthew Brettingham. He came from a long line of stonemasons, used to working on cathedrals, and this may account for much of the strength and grandeur of Holkham Hall and the Triumphal Arch.

The reason for the Arch is obscure, as it cannot be seen from the house a mile away, but possibly it served as an appetizer on the drive to the magnificence beyond. In fact, Kent's original sketch showed no windows, suggesting that his concept was purely ornamental. Brettingham obviously had more practical ideas and added windows to the finished structure.

When Nicholas Hill acquired his strange retreat, its one central room over the main archway measured approximately four by seven-and-a-half metres and had a view in either direction through Brettingham's curved windows. A stone spiral staircase led down to one of the double height rooms in the wing span to symmetrical, smaller archways. The second room had no connection to the upper room, the only access to it being via an outside door. The port corks and mussel and winkle shells found beneath the floorboards here suggest that this central room was used as a luncheon spot for shooting parties, when food was probably carried in hampers for the guests.

The task of turning it into a home would have overwhelmed even the most intrepid designers, but the inspiration of having seen a friend complete a conversion of an arch in Tyringham spurred Nicolas Hill on throughout the three years of weekend work needed to achieve his goal. The contradictions of scale – an imposing exterior with limited interior space – and the lack of water and electricity were daunting, but the new leaseholder had mains water laid on and boldly decided he could dispense with the latter modern convenience.

The massive height of the arch was in contradiction to the cramped space within, so it was decided to remove the ceiling of the central room to gain additional height in what was to be the main living room. This exposed the original roof beams, so Hill inserted sympathetic cross beams. The room below, reached by the spiral staircase, was needed for the kitchen and dining room and, as he

Left: one of the bedrooms in the east side of the Arch is furnished simply with narrow bunk beds and a wooden chest for clothes. By night, the shaded candle lights bring a glow to the warm washed walls.

wished to retain the full height, a wooden mezzanine gallery at one end was the solution. The gallery provides dressing, shower and bathroom facilities. The corresponding area on the other side of the arch has been turned into two bedrooms, which are reached by a doorway in the central arch.

Having solved the problems posed by the structural layout, Hill decided that the decorative style needed to be classical, so he collected obelisks, busts of Socrates and Alexander the Great, and Piranesi prints of other arches. All the furniture needed to be scaled to the access afforded by the spiral staircase, as the windows were even smaller and little could be carried through them. The semi-circular sofa – echoing the shape of Brettingham's windows – was made in two sections and covered in French mattress ticking. Local craftsmen made a bookcase in an obelisk shape for the living room, while nearby, architectural fragments form *objets d'art* on the desk and window sills. A great find was a folio of Matthew Brettingham's engravings for the building of Holkham.

Without electricity, Nicholas Hill then had the creative task of lighting his home by candle and oil lamps. A storm lantern from Holkham was copied and, with a nineteenth-century Finnish candlestick inside, provides the main illumination for the kitchen and dining room. Candles, with candle shades to soften the flame, light the bedrooms, and a hanging candelabra was made to his design by a local blacksmith for the main living room.

His archway retreat was intended as a weekend break from London – somewhere quiet to catch up on professional work. Somehow, though, the sheer magnificence of the surroundings makes work too mundane, and time there is spent entertaining friends or just enjoying the simple life amid the grandeur of a previous age.

Left: Nicholas Hill has designed the narrow central archway room with great skill. The curved sofa, covered in French mattress ticking, folds down to make an occasional bed for guests. The obelisk bookcase, made to his design by local craftsmen, makes use of the height without encroaching on floor space. It also partners his collection of marble obelisks arranged on the window sills. Below: two figures standing in the driveway are dwarfed by the scale of the central arch through which the carriages were driven to the Palladian grandeur of Holkham Hall beyond.

TRICIA GUILD'S CHELSEA HOME

✧

The calm exterior of Tricia Guild's home in Chelsea has not had to change with the times, but the interior is a different matter entirely. Her nostalgic Designers' Guild theme of handling fabrics extravagantly launched a fashion which took off on the mass market in the Seventies, but this style has been swept out of her own home. Elaborate curtains have been replaced with clearly defined Roman blinds, massed bunches of flowers by single blossoms and, where curves prevailed, parallel lines now define her living style.

Tricia Guild's innovative handling of fabrics launched her as an international designer. Her extravagant use of them in pastels started a rage for nostalgia which altered the look of so many homes in the Seventies. The first ranges comprised small abstract patterns, followed later by translucent watercolour effects on a larger scale. The art of her interiors lay in the apparent carelessness with which so many patterns were layered, ruched and festooned together, while her mixtures of rattan furniture and possessions, punctuated by enormous baskets of flowers (bought wholesale from the markets at Covent Garden), made unexpected corners and vistas in a home.

This complex jumble was personal to her and gave an aura of nostalgia without devotion to a specific period, but in the Eighties she threw this personal train of thought out of the window. Her love of textiles remains, but possibly her travels in Japan, plus the increasing speed of life, have eliminated clutter from her designs. Her background for life is cool and spacious, and now has clear-cut design touches.

Tricia Guild abhors a violent jerk in changing colours, especially from room to room, so she always works within a consistent colour band. Whereas pastel pinks and greens dominated her rooms in the Seventies, blue, grey and white, sharpened with etchings of black, now take over. Woven coir carpet is preferred for all the floors because it provides the textured background of a natural fibre for contemporary rugs.

The earlier version of the study/music room was designed for live piano music and as such was decorated with muted flower prints and underhangings of Victorian lace. Now there is a definite Japanese influence. Cream calico is battened flat on the walls and edged with charcoal grey, while the shape of the windows is clearly defined by Roman blinds etched with the same deep grey in horizontal bands. Patterns are used sparingly, only cushions and a throw-over for an older chair in Caroline Gray's hand-painted fabric are given space. Comfortable seating in cream calico is a must for working, reading and listening to music, though the latter is no longer produced from a piano, but a hi-tech stereo instead.

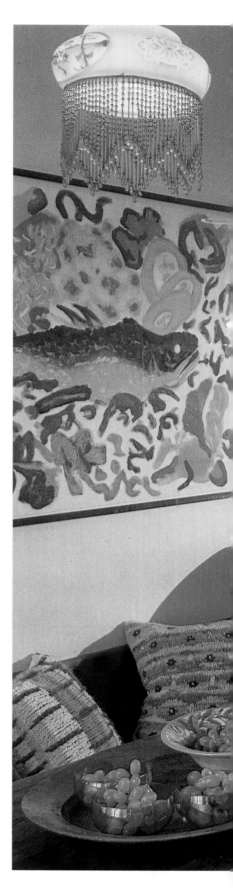

The sitting room has had a complete about-face. Where massed flowers and plants mingled with soft green and pinks and rattan furniture grouped in tight corners, the room has been swept clear, giving an aesthetically pure, cool space in which to think. Natural calico covers angular sofas and an antique armchair, while white acts as a background to grey and neutral tones, splashed with dramatic flashes of turquoise. A large lithograph by Howard Hodgkin fills one blank wall and a striped grey and white handwoven rug by Richard Wormsley follows the horizontal lines of the turquoise Roman blinds. Square glass tanks hold single blossoms of hyacinth and anemone, while hand-painted square tables in two tones of blue add to this clear-cut Eighties version of living.

The French marble fireplace in the sitting room survived the transition, along with an oil painting of a flower vase by Bill Jacklin. Hidden before by massed flowers, it is now on an equal footing with Carol McNicol's folded paper ceramic vase, which has been chosen to hold just a few lilies and soft red arctotis heads. Tricia Guild found it impossible to remove her favourite nineteenth-century landscape painting in oils, so now it

Below and bottom: the colour key for the sitting room is grey and natural white, contrasted with clear turquoise. Solid pine furniture in the kitchen (right) makes a natural background for vibrant pottery and cushions.

Building the bed into an alcove utilises all the available space in this narrow bedroom (right), and by using the same abstract pebble print to cover walls, window recesses and for the blinds (above), the sense of space is increased. A quilt cover to the same design is massed with cushions in a gentle pink and green spectrum.

Left: thick, quilted blue curtains in a giant rose design enfold the bed. These are lined in white to match the bedcover and pillow cases. Single anemone flowers fill a variety of glass bottles on the dressing table. Above: a corner in Tricia Guild's bedroom shows the matching fabric-covered walls and blinds. A white lamp casts a pool of clean light onto a table-top display by the bed.

dominates a tailored sofa, a hand-woven rug and an angular, stippled table.

Curtains have not been totally banished from her bedroom. A giant print of blue roses is battened on the walls and held by narrow grey tape, the same fabric used for the tailored Roman blinds at the shuttered windows, while the bed has a canopy hung from the ceiling by rope and is curtained in padded drapes bearing the rose design etched by quilting. The bed is totally plain, being covered in natural linen and tailored cushions. White table lamps with white pleated shades, tables covered in

plain, white fabric and blue and white china, holding just a few anemones, indicate her change of direction.

A minimal space spare bedroom has a bed half-recessed behind the return wall of another room. Wallpaper, bed and Roman blinds all have the same abstract pebble print in a shade of pink/beige, while piles of cushions are all in tailored shapes, varying slightly in their texture and prints.

Quilted-effect pink tiles have been re-used in the bathroom. In place of a soft approach with pine furniture and plants, they form the key for a Thirties bathroom.

Twin inset basins and their generous cupboards beneath are geometrically framed with these tiles, while one wall and a return corner is covered with mirrors, lit critically by banks of bare light bulbs. Roman blinds in an abstract pebble print follow the theme of straight lines.

This house is a design exercise which gives room for thought. Favourite possessions need not be jettisoned when changing course as, viewed laterally, they can be given a totally different emphasis. Contemporary art and ceramics have obviously contributed to the stimulus for the change in design. The approach is now lean and sparse, and where the criterion before was plenty, the pendulum has now swung to the minimal.

Above: patterns are used sparingly in the study-cum-music room, with Caroline Gray's hand-painted fabric used for a chair throw-over and cushion covers. Horizontal lines are the main theme, with grey chintz banding the natural calico-covered walls and sofa. Roman blinds treated in the same way define the shape of the windows.

Left: flower still life on the marble fireplace, combining Bill Jacklin's oil painting and Carol McNicol's 'folded paper' ceramic vase.

Above: the colour of the angular, stippled table is linked with a multi-coloured hand-woven rug. The nineteenth-century landscape oil painting dominates this grouping in the sitting room.

RE-CREATION OF NASH BRILLIANCE

The architect John Nash was imaginative in his conception of buildings and the imposing grandeur he left demands respect. Yet during the restoration of this Nash house, overlooking the grand arches and terraces circling Regent's Park, the owners did not allow the classic style to stifle their own ideas for a twentieth-century home.

The scale of John Nash's stucco-fronted exteriors remains a lasting influence in English architecture. From the rooftop balcony, the owners can appreciate the arches, tall buildings and inspired town-planning produced by the architect who was the mainstay of the Picturesque movement.

Above: the colours of this Italian painted chest are subtly linked with flowers on the marble top.

Above: Elizabeth Baxendale's murals make an original entrance after the classic exterior.

John Nash was an inspired town planner of the early nineteenth century. His output was prolific and in a variety of styles: Italian, castellated Gothic and even, as in the case of the Brighton Pavilion, Indian chinoiserie. The silhouettes of these buildings epitomised the Picturesque in architecture. This same combination of independent style and formality marks his greatest work, the layout of Regent's Park and Regent's Street. Indeed, his work dominates this area of London, with villas sprinkled in the Park, encircled by vast terraces and crescents of private houses.

Nash's self-confident and easy mastery of large-scale stucco exteriors led to the production of interiors on an equally grand-scale. However, when attempting to translate early-nineteenth-century interiors into homes, owners in the twentieth century can find such impressive proportions intimidating.

When Richard and Presiley Fitzgerald bought this Nash terrace house, it was obvious that the previous owners had been overwhelmed by the scale of the stairs, landings and formal rooms. Their dividing walls had halved the proportions, throwing the height of the rooms out of balance, while the landings had been littered with an odd assortment of 'cupboard' bathrooms. Clearly, before any thought could be given to interior design, all these plumbing disasters had to be ripped out, along with the partition walls, and the lost mouldings and other architectural details carefully replaced. Whilst showing a great respect for the original 1820 building, the Fitzgeralds did not allow their own flair and taste to be subdued into total acquiescence to the classical, though another Nash building – the Royal Pavilion at Brighton – provided some of the inspiration for their plans for the restoration, which took three years to complete.

The grandiose landings and entrance hall were handed over to the artist Elizabeth Baxendale for a vast exercise in mural painting. Simple outlines of cherubs, urns, laurel wreaths and classical figures, as well as portraits of the people who were involved with the restoration, combine with landscapes of flowers, trees and birds to fill the entrance and the ascending link in the house. The murals are akin to those of classical Italian villas, being designed as pictures within painted panel frames, and as such even fill odd corners – the pointed shape under the staircase is finished with a triangular frame panel. Soft peach paired with terracotta, delicate greens with blue and an overall

Above: Chinoiserie chairs are highlighted by the mirrored doors and dark setting of the dining room.

*Above: in the bedroom, blue
shaded to white is repeated in
the leaves on the wall and the
pastoral scene on the quilts.*

pale golden yellow bathe the whole area with incredible colour combinations.

Having put such emphasis on the decoration of the walls, the entrance hall floor had to be given equally important treatment, so here black and white marble draws the eye to the elegant, white staircase. This, in fact, was lacking in light, so a round, recessed window was installed halfway up the first flight, and rich moss-green carpeting was chosen for both the stairs and the upper landing. The imposing space was left bare of furniture, apart from the white Regency garden seats in the hall and a gilt painted chair and sofa at the turn of the stairs.

A less flamboyant decorative plan was followed for the rooms of the house. The treatment of colour in the drawing room has its basic shading in common with the neo-classical designs of the early eighteenth century, where the monotony of one colour in vast rooms was broken by using three tones of the same colour.

Choosing yellow, the Fitzgeralds painted the ceiling and mouldings in the palest shade, the upper walls a clear yellow and the vertical panels a tone lighter, while deepening the tones for the bottom panels and the skirtings. These tonal changes delineate architectural

Above: the roof space makes a child's attic bedroom, blending geometric and floral designs in red and white.

Above: the line-painted washstand and chair illustrate the subtle mixing of colours in the bathroom.

details, while giving a gentle setting for the pictures and mirrors displayed on the panels. Curtains of plain yellow, lined so that the light is still transmitted through the fabric, are treated quietly, with brass brackets holding them back from the classic windows. To complete this collection of yellows, a tailored pelmet is edged in a deeper yellow still.

Comfortable sofas and armchairs are upholstered in olive green with a design of pheasants, grasses and butterflies. An Italian painted chest with a marble top bears a graceful arrangement of hydrangea heads, Japanese anemones and arched sprays of berries, and an early English landscape painting and a giltwood mirror have been hung above this clever tonal grouping.

At the other end of the drawing room there is an eclectic blending of furniture and objects. A chinoiserie hexagonal table with an Art-Deco mirrored lamp on one side of the fireplace has, as a partner, a corner screen covered in early-nineteenth-century French wallpaper that depicts three allegoric figures. A curved armchair upholstered in a fine green geometric fabric is French Empire.

Double doors open on the dining room. The doors were uncovered during the removal of a dividing wall and, although they are excessively heavy as they are mirrored between the fenestration, they were left to give reflective images of the startling dark dining room. Black wallpaper with feathered sprigs of mauve and yellow lilac provides a perfect setting for the black chinoiserie dining chairs, while a large, giltwood mirror as an overmantel for the classic marble fireplace doubles the effect of the candle chandelier. To the left of the fireplace, whimsy has been allowed by the inclusion of a folded screen of

Left: a triangular framed panel under the stairs shows the creative work of Elizabeth Baxendale's brush.

architectural classic archways. This was painted by Malcolm Battersby and pinned onto a background of simulated brown marble.

Strong turquoise blue is used for the master bedroom. A large swirling pattern of leaves is shaded in blue to white for the wallpaper, and its tone is repeated for the bed quilts, which show a pastoral scene. The bed is finished with an imposing crown of soft brown drapes. A balloon back lacquered chair with mother-of-pearl inlay

Above: pale yellow suffuses the drawing room and allows the strong lines of the furniture to be seen clearly.

Above right: the painted murals ascending the staircase blend terracotta with olive green and soft peaches with warm yellow to create an inspiring colour melange.

partners an ebony table graced with brass and black candle holders.

The change of scale and shape of the attic rooms suits their more simple treatment. A child's bedroom is lined in white with red lattice wallpaper on the walls and sloping ceilings, while soft red and deep green floral chintz covers the bed and Victorian chair. The bathroom is papered in a floral design of delicate grey-green, pink and blue, and a marble-topped washstand and soft green wooden chair are both line painted to pick out all the hues of the paper.

The Fitzgeralds no longer live in this imposing Nash house, but hopefully their inspiration in drawing on other influences from the same era, and the light-hearted way in which the interior has been restored, prove that respect for an architectural period need not be an encumbrance to original design.

A DESIGN FOR ART

◆

A conventional mansion house in Surrey hides the ultra-modern flat of an artist and interior decorator. The rooms are dramatic exercises in stark black and white, the only colours being added by pictures and the occasional Persian rug. Barbara Schmalhaus' passion for other artists' work dictates that their pictures should come before decoration design is started, and not left to be hung as the finishing touches. This is an interesting reversal to the norm.

This mansion, built in 1910, was bought by developers to convert into luxury flats. It is a conservative building in London's commuter belt and, as such, you could expect to find traditional interior designs therein. Mrs Schmalhaus' flat, however, is a far cry from the grand, wisteria-clad exterior. Her interior is uncompromisingly modern in style, and if the shape of a room does not meet her criteria in design, the structure is altered – builders could be forgiven for describing her as 'exacting' when the shape of an arch or window has to be

Barbara Schmalhaus came to London to study art and progressed to running her own gallery. Since pictures need a setting, the natural development was to interior design. Here the pictures trigger the creative theme.

altered to marry with the shape of a chair. Walls have been painted white throughout and plastered smooth without a defined break at the ceilings, and, as might be expected, her love for pictures soon filled them with works by internationally famous names and contemporary young artists.

Curtains do not feature in any room, as all the windows are fitted with Luxaflex venetian blinds, enabling Mrs Schmalhaus to control the natural light. Here, in this sparse living space, she perfects her art of decorating. Deep grey carpeting throughout provides a neutral background for the paintings and furniture which dictate the colour and shapes for the design, even to the point of influencing the shape of the arched doorways. An archway was knocked through from the sitting room to the hall to enable light to flood through to the kitchen and dining room from both sides. The original fireplace is painted black, its details picked out in silver, and on the mantelpiece stands a display of Art-Deco glass. An elegant, winged sofa from Holland in black leather and chrome is placed between two black cabinets.

An angled wall that cuts the corner in the sitting room has been shaped to take a black record cabinet. Tailored sofas and footstools in natural linen provide relaxed seating at that end, while both tables in the room have plate glass tops to exhibit some carefully chosen *objets d'art*. Nests of tables in black lacquer, glass and chrome, lighting from black wall uplighters and black and chrome table lamps continue the monotone scheme, and even the cushions have been kept to black and cream linen. Colour is provided by a Patrick Procktor watercolour of Regent's Park, a crayon drawing by Mrs Schmalhaus and a gouache by Alan Davie. An Andrew Hewkin painting in strong blues hangs above the sofa.

The dining room is dominated by two lithographs by Clifford Rainey of irises, one with a blue, the other with a brick red background. An asymmetric table with rounded corners has been constructed of polished white marble and the accompanying black and white chairs have squared tops. It was Mrs Schmalhaus' request to have the outline of the chair backs repeated in the archways that caused problems for the builders, but this was finally achieved. As a finishing touch, a glass vase of yellow tulips stands boldly against the venetian blinds, while black discs shield the glare from the wall lights in this room.

Above: black leather, black lacquer, glass and chrome make aesthetic textural shapes as a setting for the focal picture. Hung above the leather and chrome sofa, this perspective painting in strong blues is by Andrew Hewkin.

Barbara Schmalhaus designed
the lacquer record cabinet to
the mitred shape of the sitting
room (above). Placed between
a pair of tailored sofas, the
angled corner displays three

artists' work: a painting of
anemones by the owner, a
landscape watercolour of
Regents Park by Patrick
Procktor, and a gouache by
Alan Davie.

From the black and white of the two previous rooms, the kitchen is an exercise in pure white. Dazzling, brick-shaped floor tiles and white table and chairs by Allmilmo moulded in semi-circles give a totally clinical air that seemingly contradicts the fact that the room is used by Mrs Schmalhaus' two children – with the family dog in tow – for sorting out their homework problems. The owner had one picture in mind for the design of the kitchen – the Michael Smith oil painting of a semi-circular piece of apple, which has been placed above the table.

The bedroom is the most dramatic room in the flat. A white bedcover, appliquéd with a geometric pattern in black quilting, faces a buttoned sofa in black moire taffeta. The radiator has been boxed in with a black, Art-

Deco-style cabinet, while the room's angled wall has been used for a black marble fireplace and mirror. An enormous painting by Andrew Hewkin of a marble-columned room with zebra-skin armchairs hangs opposite the bed, their geometric pattern facing the striking bedcover.

A room where some clutter is allowed is Barbara Schmalhaus' own work studio, but even such clutter as there is has been organised in open shelves. Elsewhere pictures even crowd into the guest cloakroom, making reflected patterns on the mirrored wall of this, the house's smallest area. In all, this is typical of the design throughout this unusual and exciting flat, which has obviously been preconceived and successfully carried out to the finest detail.

*Above: a detail of the black
and silver painted fireplace in
the sitting room. A glass bowl
of tulips and Deco glass act as
foils to the colours in the
flower painting. The
launching pad for the
bedroom design (left) was the
zebra pattern of the grouped
armchairs in Andrew
Hewkin's painting.*

*Facing page: the polished
white marble table in the
white-walled dining room
gives a clinical setting for the
pair of strong lithographs by
Clifford Rainey. A glass vase of
yellow tulips is etched against
the Venetian blinds.*

THE HOUSE AT FRENCHMAN'S CREEK

*Southern Cornwall's Helford River is one of the most romantic
waterways in England; the densely wooded banks of its estuary hide
smugglers' paths and silent inlets. Daphne du Maurier based her novel
Frenchman's Creek round one of these secret waters, and the house
known as Tremayne stands on a hill above this creek. Tremayne is a
classic Regency residence with immense charm.
There has been a house here since the fourteenth century – the present
building stands on medieval foundations and was constructed between
1810 and 1820.*

Long and low, Tremayne is a very English country house. Whilst the owners have created a heavily furnished style of decorating (few today have the time or skill to practice Victorian needlework to the extent it has been used in the decoration at Tremayne), great restraint has been shown in the treatment of the house's architectural features.

Anne Hulbert spent her wartime childhood running wild in Tremayne's wooded gardens, her tomboy activities balanced by peaceful hours learning the finer skills of needlework. After years of travelling with her husband, Dennis, their eventual return to Cornwall happened to coincide with the sale of her childhood home, and joyfully they bought Tremayne as the ideal place to bring up their three sons. An acknowledged expert on Victorian crafts, Anne set about using her fine sense of

colour and her skill in handling fabrics to create an individual decorative style for their home.

From the driveway one's first sight of Tremayne centres upon a fine Regency facade which, to one side, is graced by a floor-to-ceiling bow window. The front door opens onto a stone-flagged hallway and beyond lies a magnificent cantilevered staircase. This is lit by a tall sash window of Gothic tracery where, perched on a window bar, a collection of cranberry glass reflects shafts of deep pink onto the old rose stair carpet.

A long passage links all the rooms, from the cloaks in the original pantry close by the country kitchen, past the Edwardian dining room, to the spacious drawing room at the far end of the house. The scale of everything is wide and grand, an atmosphere enhanced by large recessed archways to the room entrances.

Each room has been decorated as a separate entity, though the colours all have a related theme, being soft or intense, but never harsh. Pastel green has been combined with a dusky pink and cream in the dining room, the drawing room is decorated in an intense blue, softened in places by pale green (to hint at the Cornish sea below the hill), while floral mixtures with underlining rose tones are found in the bedrooms, these themselves being reminiscent of country gardens.

The main drawing room fills the depth of the building, its strong blues and soft greens making it a calm and peaceful place. Deep, comfortable sofas and chairs, upholstered in a blue and green William Morris design, have been grouped about the white marble fireplace, while the recessed shuttered windows on either side of the chimney breast are dressed in sea-blue Austrian blinds. The giant bow window, flanked on either side by floor-sweeping curtains with a deep flounce, brings the green of the garden in to merge with the colours in the room. Anne Hulbert's cushion designs on the Victorian button back chairs – comprising of basket weave of different textured fabric and quilted strips – pull all the colours of the room together in delightful patterns of decreasing squares.

The formal dining room has a distinctly Edwardian tone. The wooden architrave, the mouldings to the arched recesses and the fireplace have all been painted green, as has the ceiling. In contrast to this dominant feature, the wallpaper is quiet and soft in a floral design of cream, pink and green. The ceiling moulding has been picked out in green and a delicate shell pink, while the darker

Right: the green silk shade to the brass lamp partners a green basket filled with crocus and variegated ivy. Far right: white paint is used to pick out the mouldings and door panels in the drawing room.

Left: a collection of Staffordshire figures is displayed on a round table by the bow window. Right: a general view of the drawing room. The silk Austrian blinds filter the light, increasing the blue tones of the room.

Previous page: the croquet lawn and Regency exterior of Tremayne.

tones of the mahogany table and chairs – including a dumb waiter and corner cupboard – are balanced by a sombre black and red banded fabric. A fruit trellis pattern for the curtains completes the room.

The kitchen is very definitely a country one, and a central meeting place for the family. With this fact in mind, the floor bricks, laid in a chevron pattern, have been sealed to withstand constant visits to the garden. An oversized pine table, designed for large gatherings, stands alongside permanent bench seating which is softened by cushions. The space between the bench and the high set window displays an interesting frieze of Victorian and Edwardian glazed tiles that echo the basic colour tones of the house.

Having fitted the kitchen with Victorian stripped-pine shelves and cupboards, Anne Hulbert disliked their naked appearance and chose to revert to a traditional paint finish. Using green and cream paint and adding stencilled door panels, she has created some very individual-looking kitchen furniture. Two pine cupboards were also changed: a Victorian meat safe has its door lined with an Art Nouveau fabric, while another has been painted green and its panelled doors lined with cane work. Both cupboard tops make ideal surfaces for a collection of houseplants and assorted jugs.

With a judicious use of colour, the curved doorways of the hall passage have been picked out in white against cool green walls to form elegant entrances to each room. The six panelled doors, mainly painted white – though sometimes painted in two colours to enhance the panell-

Above: the kitchen is one room Anne Hulbert did not curtain. A collection of copper and brass fills the high windowsill, with a space below for a frieze of Victorian and Edwardian tiles.

Left: the view from the dining room through to the hall. Pink and green paint pick out the detail in the coving and door mouldings in the dining room.

Left: the Edwardian-influenced dining room has an arched recess with shelves to display a collection of Staffordshire dogs and green plates. Painted in strong green and delicate pink, the intricate ceiling mouldings and wooden architraves have become the dominant features in the room.

Right: the mahogany dining table is covered with a lace cloth and holds a dumb waiter. The serving recess beside the open stone fireplace forms an alcove for a display of portraits.

Above: the Gothic windows frame a jar of salmon pink gladioli and honeysuckle. Below: detail of the Victorian needlework hanging on the drawer knobs.

Right: the workroom, where the needlework ideas for the home are born. Unusual windows give ample daylight for the intricate work.

room, these have wisely been left white. A bright baize green carpet completes the effect. Pine cupboards and drawers house all the threads, wools and fabrics used to fashion new designs for the home – Anne Hulbert is happy to pass on her skills to others and runs short courses in the art of her specialised crafts.

Some examples of Anne's intricate curtains and furnishings can be seen in the bedrooms. Roses are the Hulberts' favourite flowers and they bloom in profusion in the master bedroom. The bed is a centrepiece of needlework skill. Curtains patterned with full-blown roses and lined with a rosebud motif form a tent for a pile of individually designed cushions. The quilting and appliqué techniques used here are all based on a rose device, with the addition of the odd butterfly, while the

ing – are fitted with brass door handles and finger plates. The full splendour of the cantilevered staircase is not detracted from by its decoration. Green walls act as a foil for the white spiral stairs whose black metal filigree banisters support a curved mahogany handrail. White paint alone outlines the elegant sash window, and there are no curtains or blinds to confuse the classic forms. The only pieces of furniture are a nineteenth-century carved armchair upholstered in needlepoint and a table placed in the curve of the stairs to hold a flower arrangement. In all, this sensitive restraint in decoration has heightened the strength of the architectural design.

The needlework room is an Aladdin's cave of furnishing crafts. French doors leading into the garden have unusual hexagonal panes and, with so much activity in the

Left: a collection of antique bead embroidery cushions, with the mirror image of cushions designed by Anne Hulbert. The rose theme in the main bedroom (below) uses tiny rosebuds to full blown cabbage roses for frieze, appliqué and embroidered cushions. Right: detail of a beaded fringe to a silk lamp hanging over the dressing table.

walls are covered in a tiny rosebud paper and are completed by a frieze panel of full blooms beneath the dusky pink ceiling. An elaborately draped dressing table and a loose-covered nursing chair are graced with further evidence of Mrs Hulbert's skills.

For a guest bedroom, the colour swings back to green again. This time it is a soft moss green in a delicate pattern, and white for the walls. Most people would hesitate to handle this volume of different fabric designs in one room. A vertical patchwork makes frills for the beds, and accompanies a rose-covered quilt. Another two varying designs, banded in plain rose, have been chosen for the curtains and table covers, while fabric is also used for the light shades and another selection of cushion designs. It sounds overwhelming, yet the whole is held together throughout via a subtle control of colour.

The continuing use of varying shades of green gives a cool, calming effect to this elegant house of twenty-four rooms. It is essentially a residence devoted to specialised and original furnishing designs, and as such it makes a refreshing change to see the almost-lost art of needlework being practiced to create a comfortable, but elegant house. Though the Hulberts have now made a new home on a different scale, the calm of Tremayne will remain to beguile future generations.

Above: the ability to handle multiple patterns successfully is shown in the guest bedroom.

*Far left: three family portraits
and a collection of antique
embroidery are grouped
against rich red walls. Left: a
tweed-covered chair holds two
Hulbert design cushions,
drawing together the colour
strands in the rose pink study.
Below left: sunlight from the
front door catches the white
streptocarpus on the inlaid
table. Right: the full splendour
of the staircase is not
detracted from by furnishings.
Below: a family miscellany of
country living: looking past
the coats and hats in the
cloaks towards the calm
hallway.*

THE CRYSTALLIZATION OF A CHILDHOOD DREAM

✧

Jenny Hall's hobby as a child was decorating, and marriage and a family have not sated her appetite for interior design. This home in a terraced house in Knightsbridge bears the hallmark of her talent, gained from a prodigious number of moves. She approaches design with an assurance that has been achieved through practice and, whilst keeping a constant thread, is happy to branch off into individual concepts for different rooms.

The narrow, white-porticoed exterior (facing page) in Knightsbridge hides an illusion of space beyond, cleverly achieved by the owner through her designs. The kitchen (right) is a cool, smooth workroom. Ceramic white tiles for the floor, flush cupboards and island work surface all contribute to the clinical concept.

Designers can study, or else learn by experience. Jenny Hall started designing as a child, preferring to spend her pocket money on paint, and was lucky to have had lenient parents who allowed her to work out her ideas by decorating a loose box in the stables of their Yorkshire home.

An early marriage gave impetus to her urge to create backgrounds for living and most people would pale at her record. She has designed and lived in seventeen homes in as many years, having a penchant for turning down-at-heel buildings into civilized residences. Even a ruined cottage in Cheshire, with one wall missing so the cows wandered in and out, did not deter her, though at that stage she was new to the mechanics of restoration and decoration.

All that, though, is a thing of the past. Having perfected her skills through sixteen moves, her seventeenth house design is a gracious, white-porticoed family home in an enviable part of Knightsbridge. Acquired some years ago, when these photographs were taken, she was in the process of fining down the furnishings which, she insists, should have an 'established' look – not for her the newly decorated touch.

The standard two-rooms-to-a-floor layout of London terraced houses has been granted a generous feeling of space here by the use of mirrors to form reflective walls, while alcoves increase the depth of focus in hallways and on stairways. An overall bleached sand tone pervades to give a calm backdrop for warm russets, terracottas and faded pinks.

The usual practice of having one floor texture to increase the illusion of space is thrown out of the window by Jenny Hall. Demarcation from room to room is made by distinct changes in flooring, from matting to marble, flagstones to carpet, terracotta to gleaming white tiles – all adding to the miscellany of the individual rooms. Fireplaces also come high on her list of priorities; Hallidays in London and Oxfordshire found the right marble mantelpieces for all the main rooms, including the bedroom.

The entrance boasts a main stairway of stone, now cleaned to a pleasing cream and enriched with a nineteenth-century black and white marble floor from France, laid by the Halls, in the entrance and drawing room. The narrow hallway is expanded by a wide, pine-pillared archway to the library, which in turn leads through to the drawing room.

The adjoining drawing room is light and cool in pale creams, with one mirrored wall facing the white marble fireplace. Three comfortable sofas from Bill King are upholstered in a textured, cream coloured fabric that has a woven graph-edged pattern of soft pink, taupe and cream. Windows graced by tailored cream curtains and festoon silk blinds, both in cream, create a clean, uncluttered room. Glass and steel tables hold simple bunches of pink tulips, their curves harmonising with the bleached wooden swan.

An all-white kitchen that boasts a tiled floor and walls has a tiled 'island' as a working surface and a range of cupboards from Open Sesame. A large urn of bulbs fills the fireplace, while an indoor window box of green

Left: the reflected image of the other end of the drawing room 'doubles' the size of this elegantly furnished room.

Top: the painting of a brightly plumaged cock and hen hangs over the drawing room fireplace. Above: a generous archway leads to the library.

houseplants relieves the clinically bare lines. In sharp contrast, a cool stone bust dominates a dining room of glowing russet tones. High-backed, upholstered chairs from Peter Lyall make a comfortable circle around the table, which is beautifully lit by concealed ceiling spots directed down to fall in a pool upon it.

Corners in the stairway have been used imaginatively. An oval painting by Fernando Montes of five seated brown figures hangs above a carved pine radiator cover, while an eighteenth-century oak chest fills the space beneath the staircase, and a wooden bird is grouped with a lectern and brass candlesticks. Elsewhere, an oddly placed window is turned into an important landing by the use of smoked mirrors, pillars and a fatsia plant on a black marble pedestal, while enormously long curtains in yellow silk from Claremont and a pair of rush-seated chairs complete the effect.

A change of structural layout in the bedrooms left a narrow alcove. Jenny Hall decided to turn this into a large display recess for her favourite porcelain, and had walls and the ceiling covered in smoked glass and the space dramatically lit from above by a recessed spot.

The main bedroom has been given the warmth of spring by the use of a printed yellow fabric – again from Claremont – pleated to cover all the walls and also used for the Austrian blinds. The wall surrounding the black marble fireplace is totally mirrored, and vast bowls of bulbs add to the richness of the decoration. The bed has a valance of quilted Indian design paired with a cream quilted coverlet, and a tall ebony heron stands alongside, enhancing the rather exotic tone.

As well as collecting ornamental animals – which are scattered through the house – Jenny Hall has a vast collection of cushions to add to the comfort of life. Chairs, bed and day sofa are filled with quilted, lace-edged and frilled versions.

It is clear from the style of this house that Jenny Hall's expertise and confidence in interior design is the product of years of practical experience. Somehow, her country upbringing creeps into all the rooms, and her eye always manages to light on strange animal shapes in her acquisitive search for furniture and objects for a new decorative project.

A recess left by changing the bedroom layout has been lined with smoked mirror panels, and top lit to make a niche for an Oriental display (above). The scent of spring flowers in the bedroom (left), adds to the freshness of this 'totally' furnished room, where no space has escaped the designer's touch.

A David Hicks
Design

⟡

As David Hicks' grand-scale designs are so widely used in both private and corporate interiors, it is interesting to see his advice on a different scale. This town house in London encapsulates his polished interior design, which aims to give comfort, colour and light together with extreme elegance. It has the hallmark of his work in all mediums.

David Hicks is one of Britain's foremost designers of interiors and exteriors, and his views on design have had an immense international influence in public and private decoration since the 1950s. Much of his work is on a large scale for major corporations, hotel chains and restaurants, and he has clients throughout the world

There is a tendency for one aspect of David Hick's work to draw popular comment – his precise arrangements of objects on table tops. Possibly these 'table-scapes', which started to gain publicity in his decorating during the Seventies, are easy to imitate and so spread a vogue in design. However, the way he handles lighting and colour makes his interiors distinct. He still finds time to advise on domestic-scale rooms; this elegant town house belonging to Anthony and Jennifer Hart bears witness to the ideas of a master of polished interior design.

Lighting immediately makes an impact on the classic stone entrance, as spotlights have been directed to form a

David Hicks' mastery with light is apparent in the entrance to this elegant house. Right: versions of a wicker pattern at the formal end of the drawing room are set against plain, vibrantly coloured walls.

Left: a large mirror, framed in bleached wood elaborately carved in Gothic style, gives a view of the bedroom. Emphasis is placed on the bed by echoing the design of the wallpaper in the bedspread in a lighter tone. Facing page: more patterns are introduced into the far end of the drawing room, with the textural comfort of quilting for the sofa. The intense mustard colour of the walls and curtains is eased by glimpses of white in the draped valance, while exotic orchids draw the pink tones back into the picture.

pool on the stone steps, while in the drawing room is a mixture of patterns in tones of rich yellow and greyish blue, with tan for the carpet and a muted red fabric design for a pair of sofas. A deep claret and cream chequered fabric covers a pair of elbow chairs, while the walls are the colour of mustard flowers in full bloom.

At the other end of the drawing room, enlarged by the removal of a dividing wall, a sofa, softly quilted in a grey flower design on a geometric base, introduces a fourth pattern element. Plain curtains that exactly match the walls are lined in white for a draped valance, while a deep claret velvet covers a table by the curtains.

A tall, chamfered bookcase, made to David Hicks' design in grey-stained sycamore, is fitted in the recess of the chimney, and the fire mantel has been painted pale grey. Dusky pink orchids link some of the tones in the pattern melange, but such a mixing of patterns and colours could only have been handled by David Hicks.

After such a wealth of geometric design, the dining room has been executed in plain tones of strong colours.

Below: family photographs are displayed to effect alongside a flower arrangement on a deep claret velvet. Right: the light tones of sycamore stand in relief against the Loden green walls.

A deep Loden green, which is almost black, covers the wall above chair-rail height, and the same shade is used for the tailored curtains. Light sycamore panelling below the chair rail and a trellis of linked circles forming panels above it break the tone of the dark walls. Poppy red glazed chintz covers the circle of upholstered dining chairs, and as a final *coup de grâce* full blown parrot tulips grace the centre of the circular dining table of pale sycamore.

Floor-to-ceiling cupboards in the dressing room are also made in this attractive, soft yellow wood, as is the

dressing table. Two-directional lighting is provided by a twin-shaded reading lamp with a brass base, and brown marble and soft beige in the bathroom continues the colour scheme.

David Hicks always advocates bed-hangings, and his curtains are lined and interlined to increase both the quality of the fabric and the drape of the furnishings. Mrs Hart designed the bed for their house to have a curved sycamore headboard. One fabric design, a formal poppy head on a pattern of smaller flowers, is used in two different colourways for the wallcovering and curtains. A shade of shocking pink predominates on a pale beige ground, as does the same main tone on a cinnamon base. Bedhangings project from the wall as short wings, the headings having been finely smocked so that the fabric hangs in tiny folds.

A deep magenta glazed chintz is quilted on the bergère chair and the same fabric, in cinnamon, covers a round table. To complete the atmosphere, a carved wooden mirror has been stained with the same shades of pink and ash, and, in all, the room is a fine example of calm blending of colours and design.

ARCHITECTS' PIED A TERRE

✦

*Standing on a pocket-handkerchief plot of land, this slender house in
Hampstead, after skilfull restoration, has become a comfortable home.
Design-award furniture has been used for functional and aesthetic
pleasure in a period house with severe limitations in size.
Concentrating on one element in the conversion – wood – and choosing
outstanding pieces of furniture, the architect owners have successfully
'turned the tables' on the space handicap.*

It is difficult to visualise living in a house which has
been built on a ground area measuring four by four
metres. Subtract the brickwork and the stairway and
you come down to twelve square metres. In the hilly area
of Hampstead – fifteen kilometres from the centre of
London – the houses were built close together along
twisting lanes, and workers' homes were squeezed between elegant residences. All are now desirable properties in a district which has attracted painters, writers,
actors and architects since the days when Lord Byron
spent time there.

Before its renovation, Hollybush House had the sad,
decrepit air of the previous occupant, an old lady. Carl
Gustav Magnusson bought the house on his return from
America to head the design control of Knoll International
in London and, as an architect and designer, his solution
to the space problem was destined to be an intriguing
equation in living style.

Helped by his architect wife Emmanuela, the whole
operation was planned by Magnusson down to the last
detail. He obtained quotations from various building
companies and gave the contract to the cheapest, which
turned out to be a reputable firm suffering a rare quiet
spell. Their staff of skilled craftsmen were stumbling over
each other in restoring the tiny, narrow building – a task
which proved to be a difficult one. Wood is a material
considered by the Magnussons to have almost infinite
possibilities, so as a result it is one of the main textural
elements in their 'pillar' home. Furniture designs controlled by Magnusson have been likened to those of the
Bauhaus period in stature and the blending of this furniture with the interior of their centuries-old building was a
great challenge for the new owners.

Space dictated that passages and lobbies be eliminated, so now one enters straight into the dining room
from the street. A space to the right, beside the stairway
return wall, has been used as a library alcove, while bare,
smooth, hardwood floors with no rugs make a perfect foil
for the furniture. Cane-backed dining chairs from Thonet
by Joseph Hoffmann placed around the marble dining
table provide both comfortable seating and an economic
use of space, and a coat stand acts as a substitute cupboard for overcoats, while natural cedarwood blinds
obscure the view from the street.

The library area – which is only two-and-half-metres wide – is graced by a rich leather sofa designed by Charles Pfister and a dramatic coffee table by Gianfranco Frattini, whose design is based on Japanese peg games and aptly called 'Kioto'. Neither glue nor other fixings keep the structure together, as all the timber sections have push-in joints.

The miniscule kitchen is a compact gallery fitted with cabinets by Bulthaup that contains everything necessary for running a household. Top light is provided by the addition of a glass cupola. A wedge shape formed by the

walls of adjoining properties has been designed as an outdoor area to catch the sun and a place to prepare summer food. Whitewashed walls are offset by two yucca trees, while a metal table and chairs provide the essentials for instant use.

The rooms on every floor have uncluttered walls, while the house's narrow, winding staircase serves as an ascending gallery for a collection of posters and small pictures. Ledges above windows and the sills themselves are used to display a personal collection of model airplanes, cars, boats and trains. One exquisite, handmade Scottish locomotive has a working, wood-burning steam engine. Whilst the ground floor has bare wooden floors, the staircase and living room on the first floor have soft, cinnamon-coloured carpets that deaden sound. In the liv-

Previous page: the slender
'pillar' exterior of Hollybush
House by night.

Far left: a Frattini-designed
coffee table in the library. Left:
clear lines in the arrangement
of furniture in the sitting
room. Below: model yacht and
wood textures make an exact
still life.

ing room Mies van der Rohe chairs, ottoman and table need little additional decorative style, and the projecting bay window spanning from the ground to the second floor allows a houseplant of tree-like proportions to fill the space above furniture height.

The design of the bedroom, one more floor up, uses glass, chrome and green marble. A small recess with a mirrored wall and a marble top serves as a dressing table, while the additional floor space of the bay window gives room for a glass desk by Franco Albini accompanied by a black and chrome armchair by Paul Kjaerholm. A Gae Aulenti desklamp, some original Twenties pieces found in Parisian flea markets, including a green marble table and desk clock, and an Aubusson tapestry make this room a very individual blending of styles.

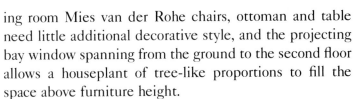

The final floor – some forty steps up from the ground floor – has a view which would be the envy of many city dwellers. It also has a bird's-eye view down to the last space-squeezing plan – a roof garden – built on the small single-storey projection to the side of Hollybush House. Reached by the windows on the first floor, this graphic outline of grey tiles surrounded by a narrow trough parapet filled with red geraniums is perhaps the ultimate proof of the success of the Magnussons' space-saving design.

Left: the 'gallery' on the staircase gives a good reason to pause and view the pictures on the steep ascent to the top of the house.

Above: a model of a classic biplane suspended beside a window, with a roof-top view of Hampstead. The architectural roof garden (left) can be seen to advantage from the top of the house.

GALLIC FLAIR IN A LONDON HOME

◆

It seems improbable that the old adage 'waste not, want not' applies to this lavish home. Yet its elegant design belies the economic cost of conversion from two run-down houses. Completed in under six months, the French owner has shown how style need not be linked to cost, as taste, imagination and immense energy – allied to a shrewd eye for a bargain – can be an alternative route to the creation of a beautiful home.

The French are renowned for being aggressive shoppers. You never see produce heaped into a bag and handed to the customer in a French market, as it is nearly always hand picked with care. The same philosophy has been held by a Frenchwoman in London during her conversion of two adjoining buildings into one family home.

Despite the fact that these houses were bought in a state of almost total disrepair, Yolande Levine's Gallic energy defied all normal timescales for repair work – she decorated a home with great style in less than six months. Her persistence and boundless energy was matched by the co-operation of her architect and team of builders, who shared her belief that nothing was impossible. Even a salvage company helped in the search for building materials urgently needed to keep the restoration work flowing, while the owner's ability to see objects in a different context and recognise quality amid dust enabled the house, which has an expensive look, to be comparatively inexpensively put together.

Mrs Levene wanted to create a home for her family which would be a calm retreat from the frenzy of city life, and the design is based on this desire. Colour is the main

Voile hung in Grecian folds as closed drapes (left) is the owner's economic method of achieving a formal elegance in her sitting room. The diffused light so created shines onto narrow floorboards and a Pleyel grand piano.

Family photographs and books line the two-storey library wall of the pine room (left).

Quilt-covered sofas and a log fire (above) make the pine room a welcoming gathering place for the family.

factor in establishing the mood; gentle tones, with no harsh accents, are all in an optimistic band of yellow, from palest cream to rich amber, the only colour change being to soft green and pink for the conservatory and one bedroom.

As the house had once been two units, some rooms are duplicated, including a pair of galleried, studio-proportioned rooms. One of these, the focal point for family, friends and dogs, is called the pine room. A magnificent floor made of narrow wooden blocks laid in a chevron pattern has been polished and left bare of any rugs. The walls are warm amber, with the lower section panelled in pine from chair-rail height. Pine panelling also covers the whole chimney breast, where there is a large mirror set in pine moulding.

A spiral staircase to the gallery stands in a corner and this area has been turned into a two storey library wall, with bookshelves from floor to ceiling. Family portraits and photographs framed in an assortment of mouldings found in markets and junk shops form a mini gallery here. Old plan chests and small blanket chests stripped to the

bare pine provide storage for games, papers and all the clutter of family life. One giant sofa and a smaller companion are covered with throw quilts made by Mrs Levene in a mixture of browns, faded blacks and muted pinks. Patchwork also covers the large floor cushions.

The other gallery room is turned into a conservatory that does not require green fingers. Silk flowers twine round cane shelves and a variety of rattan furniture is freshened by either white or green paint. Rag rugs and quilted throws in light greens and pinks soften the room. Well observed shapes group on a small white marble fireplace while a channelled pattern in the marble is echoed in the grey egg-shaped vase – found in an Oxfam shop. This has been filled with white arum lilies and stands below candle holders converted from lamps, and a pewter-framed mirror. This gallery has enough room remaining to form a green and white bedroom that has a tented curtain for privacy.

The kitchen had to be planned round an eighteenth-century piece of furniture – not a priceless antique, but a French country cupboard discovered in a junk shop. Mrs Levene found a carpenter who was able to copy the orig-

Facing page: a view from the gallery bedroom down into the 'conservatory', where white-painted wicker furniture, silk flowers and flourishing palms lend a light, airy touch.

Above: an effortless blending of the curves of a marble fireplace, an egg shaped vase and a pewter mirror – a typical example of the owner's design flair. Quilt throws, cushions and rag rugs add comfort to the cane furniture in the conservatory area (right).

Two butlers' sinks (above), married with lace curtains in the kitchen, and an antique bathtub and old Italian tiles in the bathroom (right) were all demolition finds. Soap is held on the porcelain elephant. The elegance of a stone and metal filigree staircase (facing page left) is left to speak for itself, while the spaciousness of the hall is enhanced by well-placed statues and special items of furniture. The kitchen (facing page right) suggests country living in a city home.

are thirteen of them on the front elevation alone) could have been another drain on a bank balance.

Mrs Levene, however, avoided all these pitfalls. The glory of the well-laid wooden floors has not been covered, the cantilevered staircase has remained a steady ascent of natural stone treads, and the proportions and light of the generous windows are not shrouded with elaborate curtains. Simple voile is used to make unlined drapes, hung as closed curtains on solid rods, and then held back in Grecian folds.

Space gives both the sitting and dining rooms great elegance. Furniture is placed to leave vast areas of clear floorspace. Off-white covers all the sitting-room furniture: a group of deep, cushioned sofas by the fire and, at the other end of the long room, a solitary chaise longue that stands in the midst of polished wood. A Pleyel grand piano and a French armoire increase the sense of scale. Marble statues and urns set on pedestals and a pair of

inal door and build units *in situ* to match the new to the old. As well as this, the owner of the local salvage company specialising in the rescue of architectural features from demolished buildings helped in the search for old floor tiles, pieces of marble, old floor beams – in fact anything of 'style' which could be used in the restoration. Typical of such discoveries are a pair of old porcelain sinks set side by side that make a double unit with more charm than the ubiquitous stainless steel mass-produced item. Family eating in the kitchen is round a French refectory table that has been set near to the warmth of an open fire. A pair of narrow benches and bentwood chairs add to the atmosphere of country living.

The scale of the house meant a lot of decorating. The sheer volume of rooms – the staircase covers four flights from the basement to the top floor in the central column of this extraordinary building – could have gobbled up an enormous budget, while the curtaining of windows (there

This page: two bedrooms, designed for two distinct personalities. The main bedroom (above) is a classical understatement in white, its furniture comprising restored antique 'finds' from Portobello Market. The lavish four-poster (right), constructed from garden wire and wooden posts, was the ingenious answer to a daughter's wish.

giant shells holding marble eggs set in the middle of the polished floor all keep within the off-white spectrum. Only a few soft orange cushions, Kentia palms and gilt add colour to the room.

For her daughter's bedroom, Mrs Levene's inspiration provided the desired four-poster effect at minimum cost. Garden wire threaded through lengths of pale green and pink Designers Guild fabric (bought in a sale) and secured round four wooden posts made a rapid transformation to the bed, while brass knobs set on top of the poles finished the effect. The rest of the furnishing was completed using Lloyd Loom pieces, bought in a market for a song and sprayed green with a dash of gold, and a good supply of cushions and pine chests.

In the bathroom, old Italian tiles proved cheaper than new, and their deep blue and terracotta pattern covers the

floor. An elephant stands holding the soap alongside the antique bath with gold claw feet.

The fact that Mrs Levene owned an elegant shop – Everyday Gourmet in Kensington Church Street, which sold exclusive Limoges porcelain and glassware – possibly holds the key to her attitude. The displays were amazing and so were the prices, as the pieces were manufacturers' seconds. Mrs Levine sets definite limits on the cost of an item and, if it cannot be found, uses her own invention to create the effect she desires. She shows very clearly that a large family home with enormous style does not need to be matched by an open cheque book. Street markets, junk shops and demolition firms are treasure troves of objects waiting to be found by an imaginative eye. Furnishing a house via the orthodox route of antique shops and exotic furnishings is not the only way.

One end of the living room contains just a chaise longue, an armoire cupboard and a pair of giant shells, leaving a vast stretch of bare floor. The other end (left) possesses a more intimate atmosphere. Here the grouped sofas are all kept within the room's white tones, and only tailored plain chintz cushions in grey and soft orange break the colour key.

Right: the formal dining room, which contains a large, marble-topped table laid with white porcelain. Cane-backed dining chairs, warm toned walls and Grecian-style curtains across the French doors indicate the owner's flair in creating elegant surroundings in which to dine.

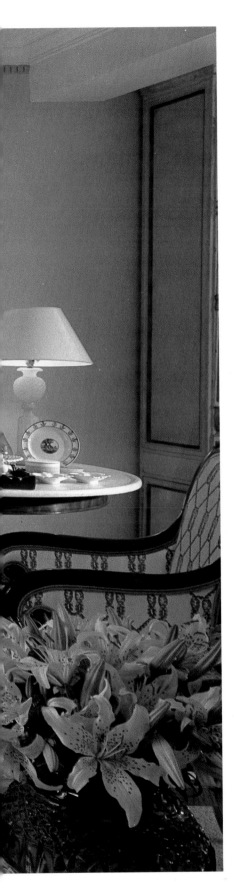

CHERISHED POSSESSIONS

The decorative theme for this early-nineteenth-century house in Cambridgeshire revolves around a personal collection of treasures. Owned by an historian who is also an antique dealer, it has been decorated to form a neutral backdrop for furniture and objects, all of them meticulously displayed according to their period and colour. In this series of mini tableaux the owner has created cameos of period style in her home in East Anglia.

The three symmetrical sash windows and curved, fan-lit door of this early-nineteenth-century house make you feel that the whole front facade could unhinge like a doll's house to reveal the rooms within. The decorative scheme within is a bland background of warm cream in which to display groupings of furniture and objects of a similar period. The sitting room fireplace was unblocked and, to re-create the elegance of the period, a marble surround was installed with a York stone hearth. A convenient open gas fire has been masked by a

In the sitting room (left), pools of light have been used to highlight arrangements of the owner's cherished possessions. The modern blanket rag rug from David Douglas provides a textural contrast to the smooth lines of the room. Right: the pride of lions on the secretaire.

copy of a Georgian grate in burnished steel from Colefax and Fowler.

The smooth sheen of an elegant pair of French Empire chairs upholstered in faded grey gingham and Regency stripe, and an imposing, dark secretaire are set against the unexpected texture of a blanket rag rug from David Douglas. A marble-top pedestal table provides a place for a delicate display of Wedgwood creamware beside a tea caddy made in pearwood and a carved tray holding a

collection of miniature ivory boxes and needle cases. When the table top is lit by the alabaster carved lamp, the whole arrangement is bathed in warm cream tones. On the other side of the fireplace a collection of ebony and marble lions has been grouped to form a 'pride' on top of the secretaire and are enhanced by the addition of a naive painting of a lion and lioness placed alongside them.

Antiques at the other end of the room are on a massive scale. An early Italian storage chest stands by a window

Low lighting in the main bedroom (below) emphasizes the luxurious textures of the room. Right: the 'dolls' house' facade of this nineteenth-century house. Paving stones laid in the front garden and set with wooden tubs make for a minimum-care terrace.

filled by a tall house lime in a large, modern pot. A French Empire chest of drawers faces a magnificent, painted bookcase with a brass-mesh front which Mrs Radford discovered in Florence. Objects, too, are scaled to the larger furniture. A pair of tall, cream marble lamp bases with black, shiny shades light a display of plates and subtly complement the strong blues in a painting of two ladies reading a book, while elsewhere passion flowers trained as a pair of formal wreaths in Chinese glazed pots support the style of three prints of French water gardens.

The dining room is less formal, though still true in its decor to the period of the house. A picture of a young lady in white muslin with a posy of country flowers in her lap greets one upon entering the room, which is furnished with a solid oak table and rush-seated country chairs on a matting floor. A recessed cupboard beside the open fireplace holds a collection of blue and white dishes.

From the very disciplined decorative scheme downstairs, there is a distinct change to feminine charm on the stairs leading to the bedrooms. Antique lace curtains draped, and not drawn, over a mahogany pole form the background for a collection of antique baskets filled with glossy-leaved houseplants. The panelled headboard in the main bedroom was made for a section of Thirties panelling and has been hung with plain calico. The bed is quilted in deep rose and stands against flower-sprigged walls. A French sofa bed with a cane back painted in faded blue is piled with antique lace cushions.

Finally, subdued tones of terracotta and mustard yellow create a restful atmosphere in the guest bedroom. Low lighting emphasises the textures of sheaves of wheat in basket stands, and those of the hand-pleated frills on the duvet covers, and the beautiful appliqué work and frills on the pillows. In all, an elegant, beautifully furnished residence of taste and style.

Right: a collection of carved ivory on a wooden tray, Wedgwood creamware and an alabaster lampbase indicates the owner's infinite patience in arranging objects.

A YOUNG DESIGNER'S BRIEF

◆

Unlike many designers, twenty-three-year-old Henrietta Newman prefers to interpret a client's ideas rather than impose her own taste upon them. Combining her youthful enthusiasm with the experience of the owner, a floral artist, she has achieved in this terraced house a result that blends the traditional elegance required by the owner with her own brand of freshness and exuberance.

Recently arrived from America, artist Polly Taylor Strauss knew the look she wanted for her terraced London home, but did not possess the practical knowledge to pull it together. Her brief to Henrietta was that she must have fresh colours to complement her flower paintings, the style should be traditional, and that she was eager to use chintz.

The basement was a shambles – an assortment of dark rooms so small that the bathroom did not even have space for a shower. The area was gutted and left as one big space for an informal sitting/dining room for everyday use, and an adjoining kitchen. A large hatchway connects the two, making the basement feel like one sunny room. Yellow in the kitchen makes it look as though the sun is permanently out, and the colour continues in the sitting/dining room, where a pair of Lloyd Loom chairs painted a creamy yellow stand either side of a painted fireplace, a brilliantly striped rag rug pulling the three elements together.

The dining table has been specially made, and flowers painted by Mrs Taylor Strauss climb up the solid base. A circular, plate glass top allows a broken colour image of the base to 'illuminate' the dining area, while, by way of a contrast to the light table, comfortable upholstered chairs

The narrow garden (above) is paved in a series of stepped terraces down to a lower, sheltered area (left) that leads into the basement dining room. Rosemary, ivy and creepers clothe the brick walls to make a green backdrop for the brightly coloured raised flowerbeds.

form a solid group, their colours balanced by frilled cushions of lattice design.

French windows, framed by cheerful, flower-sprigged curtains, open straight on to a terrace garden which is rather overshadowed, yet, by the simple device of placing white, metal garden furniture against the creeper-clad walls, the gloom is broken. Wide steps connect the lower area with an upper terrace that can be used for dining outdoors.

The formal sitting room is based on a delicate lime green and a soft pink. All the paintwork, mouldings and ceiling are white, while clear lime green has been used for the walls above the chair rail and a deeper tone for the panel below. This colour makes a marvellous setting for the owner's giltwood-framed paintings of flowers and birds.

Ebullient floral chintz curtains, draped and swagged for the valance, completely fill the wall to the garden, and the same pink-toned fabric covers the deep armchairs, but the floral theme is not allowed to spread throughout the room. A sofa and a pair of slim, winged armchairs are covered in a soft green ticking stripe to give a Regency feel, and, to emphasise the point, a pair of these chairs stands either side of a Regency card table. The room is lit by elegant, black-shaded wall lights and black- or white-shaded lamps which throw clear light by night without affecting the colour of the room. The formal air is completed by an Adam-style fireplace and an elaborate, giltwood overmantel mirror.

The main bedroom was planned round a flower painting by Polly Taylor Strauss of mixed garden flowers

Few bathrooms have such generous windows (above), so the young designer has made the most of the floor-to-ceiling curtains. Fashioned in chintz with a design of rosebud garlands and ribbons, their thickly padded hem hangs rather like a stage curtain on either side of a pink Lloyd Loom chair.

The sitting room (above) contains the Regency-style grouping of a card table and two winged armchairs covered in green ticking.

The owner's passion for chintz is given full rein in the bedroom (left), where both the extravagantly full curtains and a bedhead are covered in a large rose design.

*Above: two-toned paintwork
in the sitting room: lime green
above the white chair rail is
complemented by a deeper
shade beneath.*

*The formal sitting room (left)
is a restrained blend of dusky
pink and cool green. The
elaborate filigree scrolls on the
giltwood over-mantel mirror
are matched by the swagged
valance hung above the
"wall" of curtains overlooking
the garden terrace.*

tied with a large bow. The owner's passion for chintz has been allowed full rein, so roses and blue flowers in a traditional English-garden design have been used for the curtains at the ceiling-to-floor sash windows, and this design covers the bedhead too. Secured by fabric ties, the curtain valance is swagged and held with red rosettes, while the same shade of red lines the falling drapes at either side.

A co-ordinated fabric of a quieter design – pale pink garlanded roses – is used for the curtains in the adjoining bathroom. Interestingly, their hem has been padded so that they swell out from their restraining tie-backs, while the hem of the valance (made this time as a deep, flat pelmet), is padded and scalloped, and the garlands of roses in the design shown as a flat fabric. This padded

hem makes a soft yet imposing treatment of the long window, while a gentle green for the wall and an equally delicate tone of pink for the carpet and Lloyd Loom armchair sensitively links these colours.

From this there is a jolt to another window where the curtains, made to a design by Polly Taylor Strauss, set the stage for the view of a neighbour's conservatory. They are made as an orange and lemon fantasy in plain fabric with braid edging. Outside, a red front door echoes the shade of the geraniums in the window box, and adds a fresh, bright note to the white-painted brickwork.

Judging from the results of this particular commission, Henrietta Newman's ability to visualize and interpret the customer's basic ideas so successfully, will bring her many more challenges in the future.

A brilliant red door (below) and scarlet window box geraniums – typical of the zestful approach of Henrietta Newman – stand out beyond a black-and-white tiled entrance and smart black street railings.

Above: an exuberant combination of yellow-painted Lloyd Loom chairs and a rainbow-hued rag rug in the sitting/dining room. Shades of yellow are used with grey to pick out the panels on the recessed cupboards, and yellow also makes a cheerful contribution in the dark terrace garden (facing page).

STYLE ON A SHOESTRING

◆

Given an open-ended budget and no time restrictions, the choice for style is limitless. But within a tight framework on both counts the solution is not so simple. The cost of redecorating a run-down property can mean a financial problem after completion of the purchase. When a strict budget and time limits control style, it takes inventive design to meet repairs and make an apartment with presence. Here, simulating age with paint techniques is one interior designer's solution.

By employing interior designer John Russell, both the budget and the time limit of three months for completion of the work were achieved for the owner of this flat. The rooms had excellent proportions, but the fifteen-foot-tall windows needed an excessive amount of fabric to curtain them. However, on finding the original wooden shutters in good order, the designer decided he would create the mood of a cobwebby Italian palazzo.

A pair of tall, purpose-built bookcases stand either side of the fireplace, and two round columns make a dining area at one side of the living room. The genuine cobwebs of the run-down flat were then 'transferred' via fantasy painting techniques to 'age' the mouldings, the edges of the walls and the carvings on the fireplace, also transforming the stark new pillars into cracked marble columns. The overall effect was an instantaneous change of style.

The carpeting and furnishings are all limited to the aged tones of the marbled paintwork, leaving a pair of red upholstered chairs by the fire as the only strong colour here. A grand piano adds to the presence of the room, while the columned dining area is positively theatrical, particularly at night. An oversize mirror reflects a custom built dining suite. Made in Brussels in the style of Louis XVI, the oval dining table has red plush upholstered seats with cane backs, and above it hangs an elegant chandelier. Massed flowers on a corner cupboard add a warm splash of colour to this 'aged' room.

Lighting used effectively is a great creator of mood. Banks of spotlights set above the false ceiling mouldings delineate the column and fresco designs, and at the same time accent the height of this room. Several table lamps with neutral shades make pools of light without creating a colour disturbance in this generally quiet-toned room, while a gypsophila tree in a blue and white vase is lit from below to get the maximum effect from the filigree of its branches.

Having achieved an effective statement of style in the living room, the kitchen, with its ancient plumbing to hide, was not to be quite so easy. Tall units from a range of white and grey-trim cupboards from Ultrachoice maximised the height of the room, while curved corner units made the best use of the available floor space.

The master bedroom and bathroom are decorated in more conventional style, but the spare bedroom – which doubles as a study – again makes full use of paint techniques for economic, though stylish, effects. Here the walls have been sponge-painted in two shades of green, and the tall windows curtained in cream watered taffeta. The space occupied by a very tall cupboard has been broken by outlining its twelve door panels in a shade of soft apricot that contrasts with its cream base colour. Left as a single tone in a small room it would have been overbearing alongside such a long fabric drop of the same colour.

Whilst not maintaining a cohesive style throughout, this apartment does illustrate what can be achieved when restoring a property within a budget when time is of the essence.

An ice bucket filled with summer lilies placed alongside a large Taiwanese plate (below) makes a simple but impressive arrangement on a rosewood chest of drawers in the living room.

Simulated age paint techniques give the columned recess of the dining area (facing page) the classic style that John Russell required for his design. The strategically placed mirror adds to the grandiose scheme, as do the chandelier and a candelabra on a tripod table.

Right: a print by the American artist Robert Motherwell (right) hangs alongside a gypsophila tree made by John Russell. The Louis XVI-style sideboard is part of a dining suite made in Brussels. The corner details of the walls in the living room (facing page) and the fireplace have been 'aged' to give presence to the room. All the colours in this room – apart from the red open armchairs either side of the fire – fall within the tones of the marbled paintwork. The marble capital of a pillar makes a solid base for a glass-topped table for another red focus of roses and lilies.

A RESTORED GEORGIAN HOME IN LONDON

When a team of experts were called in by the owners of this house in north London, they were keen that architectural cohesion should come first to realign the two periods of the building. A magical verandah terrace now links the first floor to the garden and, with the help of a group of craftsmen, the interior design has been handled sensitively to make it a personal family home with great charm.

The design of the balcony terrace (facing page) links parts of the house, as well a linking the house to the garden, thereby offering access from several rooms direct to the lawn (above).

Christopher Smallwood was asked if he could rescue this 'find'. It was an architect's dream – a double fronted Georgian house which was originally single fronted, the later addition never having been aligned externally or internally. The proud new owners were content to camp with their family on the top floor, while their architect set about his remedy, which was achieved within one year.

Windows and doors were a main priority. Matching window rails and sills were replaced on the street facade, and a large front door, set centrally, now opens into a generous hall-cum-family sitting room instead of the former gloomy passage. Double mahogany doors connect on either side to a kitchen and the drawing room, allowing easy circulation for family living.

The rooms on all floors lacked light and air, so airiness and symmetry became the key to his transformation. A concrete floor at varying levels on the ground floor was replaced with mahogany boards from Brazil, ordered in random sizes so that they could settle out of line. Dowels, which appear to fasten the boards, merely conceal screw

Re-aligned window rails and sills and a central front door (above) give the Georgian front elevation a unified appearance.

The verandah terrace (above) is protected by a long white awning edged in green. The drawing room (far right) has windows at either end, overlooking the garden terrace and street. The room's walls are covered with a cream fabric by Pallu and Lake and finished with picot-edged petersham. The Kingcome sofas are covered in chintz of a soft red-brown Indian design from David Ison Designs.

fastenings into the joists, while the aged quality of the boards was accomplished by allowing the new floor to be trampled by the workmen's heavy boots. When the craftsmen departed each night, the floor was swept and waxed, and the tramping cycle repeated the next day. The worn, gentle sheen of 'age' gives a welcoming glow to the main living room.

The fenestration at the rear of the house needed a complete facelift. A rotten wooden platform outside the kitchen, balanced precariously over the basement area, meant that anyone stepping out through the drawing room window faced a sheer drop to the garden below. Christopher Smallwood replaced the ill-matched casement windows with a sashed Georgian window to the staircase, and hung a pair of arched French doors on either side to both the kitchen and drawing room.

He then designed a grandiose terrace verandah with a wide central staircase leading down to the garden. The staircase was cast in Wales and painted deep green. The kitchen and drawing room both have a garden terrace area for eating outdoors, shaded from the sun and the chill evening air by a long white awning bordered in green. Viewed from above, the tiny garden has a curved stage laid in yellow bricks at the foot of the iron staircase, with a pocket handkerchief lawn edged with flagstones. Raised brick beds, filled with impatiens and geraniums, have lattice fencing behind them for a variety of climbing plants to enclose the garden.

The curved brick stage then turns behind the staircase in a series of brick steps to a lower terrace outside the basement flat. The brick exterior of the house has been

Right: a collection of silver-framed family photos stand with a massed bunch of garden flowers in the drawing room.

painted white here to make a light, secluded patio area on either side of the iron staircase, which has easy access from three French doors. Large terracotta pots of trailing geraniums and white daises give instant colour in a garden that requires hardly any work; the tubs can be replenished with bulbs and evergreens to give shape and colour all year round.

Having had both the structure and the layout for the garden perfected by their architect, the next stroke of beginner's luck for the owners was finding Nina Campbell, who has immense flair in the handling of fabrics. She supplied all textiles for the house and, in turn, introduced them to a flamboyant curtain designer, Len Carter, who encouraged the owners to be extravagant with fabric.

The windows, which the architect took such care to get right in the restoration, have all been dressed distinctively, each one projecting a different tableau of the terrace garden and drawing the house and the garden closer together. Pink, candy-striped taffeta, heavily flounced for the staircase sash window, makes a framed 'picture' with a window box of pink geraniums.

The generous hall-cum-family sitting room (left) has mahogany double doors on either side of it leading to the kitchen and drawing room, thereby facilitating the freedom of movement demanded by family living. A reflection of this room in the mirror above the open fire (right) shows a screen hung with a collection of Paisley shawls in the archway to the drawing room. Top right: favourite cat ornaments are grouped beside dishes and a lamp with a pleated shade on a black and amber papier mâché tray.

covered with a cream fabric 'Argyle' by Paullu and Lake, finished with apricot-edged petersham ribbon, while the Kingcome sofas are covered in chintz printed with an Indian design in a soft, reddish brown by David Ison Designs. Sofas ordered from Brian Kingcome are made to measure – depth and height are adjusted to each client's leg length for the ultimate in comfort.

The kitchen is unobtrusive, with painted pine cupboards and a solid, scrubbed pine table. Two pairs of French cane-backed chairs were found at Geoffrey Bennison's shop, and the generously draped curtains echo this cane pattern, while the open French windows are a constant invitation to enjoy the garden.

Inspiration in design comes from unexpected sources. The idea for the decoration of the bed in the master bedroom was sparked by something seen by Christopher Smallwood in a Mexican hotel brochure, which he describes as 'Raffles Colonial' and commissioned from a Wiltshire craftsman. Made in maple wood, it is hung in a froth of white organdie, edged with scalloped lace and covered with lace pillows and wool rugs. A French bergere chair upholstered in pale blue in the bedroom is filled by exquisite cushions made from silk applique and seed pearl embroidered lace, and finished with a silk shawl thrown over the back of it as a headrest. Soft blue curtains printed with bunches of violas finish the gentle decoration of the bedroom.

A Victorian nursing chair in the bathroom is upholstered in 'Madam Elizabeth' striped flower chintz by Claremont, and the same design in organdie has been used for the soft Austrian blinds. Another window has cream glazed curtains, printed with soft red roses and blue leaves, and plain blue is then used to edge the draped valance caught by self-coloured bows.

A Regency day bed in the children's room has tented drapes copied from the book *Girls and Boys*. A print of fine, pink rosebuds on cream cotton is used to line quilted drapes of a fine dot pattern, hung over a bar, and then tented over the ends of the day bed. The same fabric is used to upholster a Victorian button back chair.

As well as making the one-off design for the master bedroom, Nick Holgate also made the table and chairs for the terrace. Fashioned in teak, these have wooden lattice backs with squab cushions covered in a peony print.

The whole house has been designed for maximum access to and from every room, as well as to the garden.

Carnation-sprigged cotton for the kitchen terrace, peony red corded cotton for the drawing room, and a frivolity of white organdie for the master bedroom give the house a joyous air.

The house has been designed as a family home, which is obvious as soon as you enter. A circular table in the sitting room is a favourite display area for books, boxes and family photographs. The owners are not shy in displaying these, they fill many corners in their home – even the inside of cupboard doors are covered in them – while library recesses on either side of the fireplace hold books and mementos of family life, beside bowls of country flowers. A large mirror fills the wall above the fireplace and gives an image of the arch, reduced in scale by a screen hung with antique paisley shawls. The walls of this room are drag painted in creams, with deep grey curtains and armchairs corded in burgundy.

The drawing room has windows at either end overlooking the garden terrace and street. The walls are

Left: a Victorian nursing chair in the bathroom, upholstered in 'Madame Elizabeth' striped flower chintz by Claremont. The same design, in organdie, is used for the ruched blinds. The stairway sashed window (facing page), hung with striped taffeta curtains, forms an ebullient frame for the garden.

Above: Len Carter's curtain designs for an upstairs window. The tented bed (below) was copied from a children's book Girls and Boys.

Although a great mixture of fabrics and patterns have been used, there is no hint of over-decoration – instead they give an ebullient air to this residence, while Geoffrey Bennison and Portmeirion provided a treasure trove for the owners' individual taste for antiques. Uptown junk was also bought with a discerning eye and transformed by Len Carter's art with fabrics. Owners who call in a team of professionals sometimes live in a designed 'house'. The owners did not fall into this trap. Although new to the game, they found they were instinctive decorators and have created a visual joy and a delightful family home to share with friends.

Above: a blue and white winged armchair in the bedroom, draped with a fringed shawl and filled with silk appliquéd and seed pearl embroidered lace cushions. The master bedroom (left) and adjoining bathroom are linked by the fabric choice: the French chair is upholstered in blue and white spotted muslin to match the bathroom walls, while the Mexican-inspired bed (right) is hung with a froth of organdy edged with lace.

THE ENIGMA OF A LUTYENS-INFLUENCED HOME

❖

When it was acquired in 1926, the new owners of this house considered the interior too modern for their accustomed style of living, and indeed, on first appearance, the home of the Dormer family presents an architectural mystery. The building, designed by Sir Oswald Partridge Milne in 1907, is large, but has no pretensions to grandeur – though it hints at an earlier period with its leaded, Tudor-style windows. The Dormer family decided to remould the character of the house with seventeenth-century artifacts from other buildings, and this design remains the same today.

Left: filtered by leaded windows, shafts of light strike the octagonal table and the Charles II leather armchairs of the dining room. Right: the brick archway to the front door, framed by a large camellia and a wisteria.

Left: mellow panelling makes a corner setting for a collection of glass, while (right) the open ecclesiastical Gothic doors, set into a stone archway in the library, give a glimpse of the barrel-vaulted hall.

Bookshelves recessed into the wall panelling (below) enhance a quiet reading corner in the drawing room.

Above: a still life of past sporting activity in a passage painted deep saffron yellow.

Sir Oswald Partridge Milne was a partner of the famous Sir Edwin Lutyens, so, not surprisingly, the building has the attributes of the latter's plain, balanced style. The windows are not of the turn-of-the-century original design, having been added twenty years later, when the Dormer family bought the property. As they had always lived in large, period houses, the Lutyens-influenced house was far too modern for them, so they had the fenestrations changed to leaded Tudor-style windows, and certainly, the light cast from these does have a dramatic effect on the atmosphere of the rooms.

The urge to re-create an earlier period set in train a virtual re-construction of the interior design. With the advice of Partridge of Bond Street and the decorating firm Trollope, Mrs Dormer's compelling interest was to find the correct artifacts to remould the character of the house.

Fluctuating fortunes of far larger and older properties aided the task. Seventeenth-century panelling for the

Bookshelves, conveniently set above the silk headboard in the main bedroom (below), offer a wide choice of reading matter.

dining room was bought from the Yorkshire estate of Middleton Hall, while a Yorkshire ecclesiastical building parted with a pair of Gothic doors, which were fitted in the stone library archway. A fireplace in the drawing room was discovered at Milton Abbey, and the structure of the hall ceiling was changed to a barrel-vaulted shape. From the Edwardian exterior you would not expect this interior to possess the atmosphere of a small Gothic castle.

The present owners, Daphne and Michael Dormer, inherited the house on the death of Mr Dormer's mother, who had inspired the transformation of style. The home was so instilled with atmosphere that they had no wish to alter the decoration. They did, however, change some of the colours of the walls, but in a refreshing sense, rather than in a wish to follow vogue.

Not only did the Dormers move into a home full of early ancestral portraits and steeped in family history, but into a house that also holds memories of the famous people who spent time there during World War II. Michael Dormer's mother was hostess to the Norwegian royal family for two years and, during their official residence, leading world figures visited the house.

The Dormers have obvious pride in this association. The King of Norway spent hours in the sitting room at the desk which stands in the window recess, and he received other visiting royalty, including the Queen of Holland and the King of Yugoslavia. Military figures also came to the house, such General de Gaulle from his London headquarters, while the British field marshals Montgomery and Alexander planned their offensive on North Africa and the combined landings here. The house

Left: silk embroidery covers a round table (left), upon which stands a collection of miniature portraits. A sparsely furnished bedroom (right) caters for the comfort of guests.

covers an epoch in history based round the early years of this century, yet the style and furnishings come from earlier decades.

The mellow, panelled dining room invites quiet decoration. You are hardly aware of the furnishings, as the light streaming in through the re-designed windows onto the shining furniture sets the atmosphere. A long, hexagonal table of polished wood glows when laid with silver and glass, the leather armchairs, made with spiral turned legs in the reign of Charles II, are still upholstered in their original green leather, and their bold, embossed gilt pattern gleams above the table, to be echoed in the strong flower design of the gold and yellow dinner service.

Portraits of the Dormer ancestors hang in the vaulted hall, including those of Robert Dormer, the 1st Earl of Caernarvon, Charles Dormer, who was Viscount Astor, and the 3rd Earl of Bute.

The stone fireplace is surrounded by decorated wood panelling and in front of it stands a tapestry firescreen, while the stone arched doorway and Gothic doors make a fitting entrance to a library lined with leather-bound volumes of English and French heraldic books from the eighteenth and nineteenth centuries. Family memories fill the room; there is a special book containing nature studies, executed (at the tender age of fourteen) by the great grandfather of the present owner, which lies open on a round table. All the furniture in the room is of the seventeenth century, with the exception of a tall bookcase made by the present owner. This has been sponge painted in rich browns to blend in with the aged pieces, such as a large Italian marriage chest. Two tapestry-covered chairs stand on either side of this heavily carved piece, while steel wall brackets hold six parchment lights and complete the antique group.

In the primrose painted study, an unusual collection of decorative French books fills the recess by the Louis XVI fireplace. The furniture for the house was all collected by Michael Dormer's mother during the late Twenties. Chosen for comfort and discreet elegance, the faded brocades covering the sofas and chairs give an air of great charm to the panelled room. Collections of family engravings, miniatures, snuff boxes and fruitwood tea caddies are arranged on various tables in the drawing room with unself-conscious ease, while in an alcove by the windows book shelves have been set into the wood

Above: the desk in the drawing room used by royal visitors, (left) a wider view of this room, where faded brocades merge with the panelled walls, and (below) a group of family portraits in the vaulted hall.

The exterior of the house (left), built at the turn of this century, is alien to the atmosphere within. Shelves recessed on either side of the Louis XVI fireplace in the yellow study (facing page) hold a decorative collection of early-nineteenth-century books.

The kitchen (below left) makes no concessions to modernity.

panelling. Diffused light from the leaded windows and warm, low light from table lamps evokes an atmosphere of relaxation and peace.

Pink-washed walls liven the gun room, where a collection of French sporting pictures and a miscellany of canes and umbrellas are displayed. Another part of the house has deep saffron walls and here sports equipment

has been left as though a game of badminton had just been played.

The house has an air of time arrested, and seems far removed from the pressures of the late twentieth century. The present owners' only concession to updating the kitchen has been to warm the room's white tiles with the addition of sponged peach walls. In the bathroom the Victorian cast-iron bath stands impressively on claw feet, and there is a generous hand basin set in marble. Large, square ceramic tiles cover the walls, and a bell push hangs within reach of the bath to summon the servants who once looked after the house.

The guest bedroom probably illustrates the lifestyle here more clearly than any other room. Everything is laid out for comfort to welcome guests. An open fireplace with brass fender has a wooden scuttle piled with coal for a warming fire to be lit. The room is full of books and collections of magazines, a teapot stands on a porcelain warmer, while the large bed, covered in ivory brocade, has an embroidered bell pull above the padded headboard. Faded Oriental carpets, ivory satin striped wallpaper and rich red sateen curtains all combine to make a quiet, comfortable background.

Few houses of this age have withstood the changing pendulum of overt decoration, but, after all, the English country gentleman did not wish to move with the times and, once he was content with his residence, it stayed as it was. It is the sort of household encountered in English country houses where taste was endemic.

FROM REGENCY COACH HOUSE TO HOME

Mr and Mrs Lindsay Masters have made an inspired and imaginative transformation of a former coach house into a classic country home. Nothing has been done to damage the architectural integrity of a practical building, while some strikingly unusual artifacts rescued from demolished buildings have been incorporated into the interior design, and original ideas used for treating surfaces.

Sweet-smelling stephanotis and passion flowers grow in an organised tangle in the conservatory (left).

Above: the classic symmetry of a home that was originally built to house coaches and horses.

Buildings which change their use so dramatically hold a special fascination. School and chapel conversions are commonplace, but a coach house into a home is unusual. The coachman, who no doubt drove his charges back at a spanking trot round the circular drive, would not have expected to find children's bunks in the horse stalls, or a drawing room where the carriage stood, but such is the case after the coach house's transformation into this elegant home. The owners have left much of the basic structure intact, using the dignity of the early-nineteenth-century windows and doors as a central feature in the conversion.

The original arched entrance has a recessed lobby with double doors opening on to a flagged entrance hall. The space has been treated with utmost simplicity: the brick walls have been left unplastered and painted with two coats of differing honey tones, the rough texture catching the colours unevenly to give a broken effect.

A straight, simple staircase connects the ground and first floors, with an arched door beneath leading to the garden. The massive space is balanced with an impressive, seventeenth-century country table, and all new entrances have been fitted with double doors and arched architraves to echo the window design. Two yucca trees standing either side of one doorway, and a pair of lamps set in the windows either side of the front door are the only other objects in the room.

The drawing room runs the full depth of the house. Here Marisa Masters' brilliant idea of having two-tone stained floorboards provides almost all the decoration needed for this gracious room, and the concept is repeated in the wooden fire surround. The rough brickwork of the coach house was plastered, but then the owners had the courage to leave the pink walls and ceiling in their neutral, plaster-coloured state, making a quiet,

Above: the elaborately carved side cupboard which divides the kitchen from the dining room. The kitchen (facing page) is a practical family room with space to prepare and enjoy good food. The garden provides an abundance of produce – bowls of vegetables are used for decoration in place of flowers.

By the addition of legs and a plate glass top, imagination has turned the arched porticos from a chapel into a magnificent table (right). The lighting is provided by a medieval castle fitting.

This narrow bedroom (facing page top), papered in fine Laura Ashley design, is almost completely filled with a Jacobean carved bed. A pair of English oak chairs set either side of it and concealed ceiling lighting create a centre stage effect. The original horse stalls (facing page bottom) serve as a dormitory. The stalls are just wide enough to hold beds, which are covered in Mary Quant bed linen of a design that accentuates the groove lines in the panelling.

The master bedroom (above) centres round an intricately carved bedhead – once a rotting choirstall that was rescued and lovingly restored. The bedcover is a copy of an old Italian design found in a street market in Siena. The wallpaper is based on a sixteenth-century Turkish design from Osborne and Little. Right: understated decoration in another bedroom, based on contrast tones of brown. Amber-painted walls act as a foil for a dominant chevron fabric.

textural background for the dominant floor. Arches made on either side of the fireplace lead into an enchanting conservatory room.

Furnished with white metal furniture and a pair of white-upholstered sofas on the one solid wall, the rest of the room appears to consist of arched French windows leading to the garden. Whilst there are large palms, camellias, oleanders and lemon and orange trees, most of the greenery is trained up the walls and over the ceiling to make a deliberate tangle of exotic plants. *Ipomea learii* creeper entwines with sweet-smelling stephanotis and passion flowers to form trellis 'curtains' to the arches that lead through to the drawing room.

The ability to put strange objects to good use in decorating gives a room its individual stamp. Mrs Masters found two arched porticos from a chapel in a junk shop. They were bought for a song and, with the addition of legs and a plate glass top, make a magnificent table for the dining room. The lighting here emanates from a medieval castle fitting, and with high-backed oak chairs and the two-tone, brown-stained floor, the only other decorations are deep brown curtains with a chevron stripe.

The kitchen is a practical family room whose work surfaces are all marble, with simple shelves suspended by chains so all the cooking ingredients are near to hand. The walls have been left as rough plaster, the ceiling painted baize green and a matching roller blind added to the lovely, curved window. Three counter-weighted lights – two for the sink and working surface, and a larger, simple, white metal shade above the table – give soft, direct light at night, and, as in the conservatory, the stone-

flagged floor gives a gentle sheen. The family grow all their own vegetables and these are a source of pride – so much so that they are used for decoration as well; a bowl of fresh produce, rather than flowers, is often used on the elaborately carved pine side cupboard, which has been placed as a dividing wall between kitchen and dining room.

Throughout this conversion, the owners have exercised great control in their use of the available space. Nothing of the original architecture has been destroyed, while they have kept the furnishings to a minimum so that the grace of the building is not hidden.

The original wooden stalls for the carriage horses have been left alone – even the timber chewed by a bored inmate remains. They have been painted matt brown to make sleeping 'bays' for a fluctuating household, while the loft at one end, probably initially a hay store, makes another balcony bedroom. A pine Welsh dresser under the balcony holds a collection of Staffordshire china cats and Adams china.

The archway from the conservatory to the library is obscured by luxuriant foliage (left). Large sofas ensure that the conservatory is used as a living room, rather than just as an area for growing plants.

Understatement in the hall (below) accentuates the original structure. Here rough brick walls are painted in two tones, while the stone-flagged floor has been left bare, with just a large, seventeenth-century pine refectory table to give scale. The archway, flanked by a pair of yucca trees, leads into the drawing room.

The master bedroom centres round the intricately carved headboard, which was lovingly restored, treated and pieced together from a rotting choirstall, and this is complemented by the bedcover, a copy of an old Italian design found in a street market in Sienna. Not afraid to leave surfaces in the raw state, the Masters had the ceiling plastered in a cheap, grey variety of plaster and then carefully swished it with a paintbrush before it was allowed to dry. Now it possesses a velvety texture that offsets the richly patterned green and red wallpaper, based on a sixteenth-century Turkish design. A pair of ornately carved wooden chairs stand in solitary isolation, while outside a metal balustrade rescued from a demolished house has been added as a balcony for the bedroom over the conservatory roof.

On a smaller scale, another bedroom has the walls covered in a warm brown, finely patterned, Laura Ashley paper matched to a plain, self-tone carpet. The width of the room is filled by a carved Jacobean bed, there being only enough space either side for a pair of English oak chairs. Just two spotlights set in the ceiling light the bed and bring out the detail of the carved wood. Instead of the ubiquitous wash hand unit, a simple, brown ceramic basin stands on bare wooden balustrades, once part of a staircase.

The owners have shown enormous restraint throughout the interior to preserve its architectural integrity. So often with conversions to domestic use, much of the original structure is permanently lost in the process, but here individual imagination and sensitivity has been applied to create an elegant home from a practical building.

The brilliant idea of two-toned floorboards (above) provides almost all the decoration needed for this elegant room. A curtain of greenery divides the sitting room from the conservatory.

Wrought iron found on a demolition site forms a balcony to a bedroom over the conservatory (right).

TRANSFORMATION OF THREE ARMY GARAGES

Incisive action has rescued a muddled collection of garage buildings in the peaceful area of Hampstead. Although he has no training in architecture, Bob McLaren took on the challenge of turning them into a creative living space, in the process demonstrating what can be achieved with the most unlikely structures using radical design.

Bob McLaren's concept for these garages meant the integration of the house and rear garden through the winter garden room. This room leads directly onto a series of stepped-up flower beds built in grey brick (right). His colour control extends to the garden (left) allowing just grey, green, red and white.

It could be said that these abandoned army garages in a placid Hampstead road have been given architectural 'electric shock' treatment. Bought on a whim, the three empty garages – constructed over a period of time like an ill-assorted jigsaw puzzle – appealed to McLaren's incisive vision. He instantly recognised the potential of the buildings and his basic plan – kitchen leading into the garden, a two-storey-high garage sliced in two, spaces left open, and renewed use of the existing chimney – was formed within minutes of seeing the site and never essentially changed.

The garages adjoined a large lodge – once General de Gaulle's London headquarters and afterwards used by the British Army – and had little pretension to architectural integrity, comprising seven different levels and having an exterior covered in that

curiously English surface 'pebbledash' – pebbles set in cement.

Bob McLaren had the entire structure gutted, the ghastly surface chipped off, and the whole building re-rendered. He retained a few redeeming architectural features, keeping some of the gables but lopping ten centimetres off the bottom of the strange, Swiss-chalet-like overhang. He also kept the top half of a ventilation window in the two-storey garage, converting it into double doors to reach a deck built to overlook the summer garden at the rear of the house. He aligned the roof levels with a 'bridge' of sloping skylights to light the main area of the house and provide relief from the overbearing gables. All interior walls are painted pale grey and partnered by only two other colours throughout the house – warm burnt orange in the master bedroom and brilliant vermilion red in the kitchen. One level was drawn as a constant horizontal line through this house of many levels – walls, working services, mantelpieces and stair rails are all at exactly the same height from the floor, providing continuity in this open-plan living space. Bob McLaren hates doors and dispensed with them everywhere except at the entrances to bedrooms and bathrooms.

The decor is a skilful combination of a functional, contemporary style and lacquered Art Deco. The house is littered with chairs designed by Mies Van der Rohe, Gerritt Rietveldt, Bruno Mathesson, Gerald Summers, Marcel Breuer and Adrienne Gorska, all of which are in perfect harmony with those of Charles Eames. Equally at home are some fine Art Deco pieces, including a magnificent Sue et Mare inlaid cabinet which has prime place in the dining room. Here, the table, a black and chrome prototype of Rene Herbst, has been paired with a curved chrome seat, another early prototype designed by Adrienne Gorska.

Grey chevron entrance gates slashed with red (facing page bottom) prepare the visitor for McLaren's Coach House. The front garden, hidden behind the high grey brick walls, was treated as a pseudo-Japanese water garden, complete with lily ponds and grey granite stone. The arch of Mucha's Medee (facing page top) reflects the arch of an original coach house window which now leads onto the deck over the winter garden.

Below: the brick and tile barbecue in the garden. The original ventilation chimney was rescued from the roof of the coach house.

A colourful collection of graphics – original posters by Lautrec, Mucha, Cassandra, Kiffer, McKnight-Kauffer, Gesmar, Grasset and others – punctuate the cool grey walls. Mistinguett by Gesmar faces a powerful likeness of Maurice Chevalier by Kiffer. Etchings by Magritte and Picasso, and a collection of Raoul Dufy's original fabric designs created for Bianchini-Ferier, the famous Lyons silk manufacturer, compete elegantly for attention.

This collection of early twentieth-century design in the living area is seen from the stairs, while the chef gets a counter-top view of the dining area from the kitchen, half a flight of stairs above. The kitchen itself is a large, efficient and open work space. Everything is functional and chosen for its clean lines, and throughout, pale grey is contrasted with vermilion venetian blinds and diagonally striped tiles. The kitchen opens onto an evergreen courtyard, close to a brick-and-tile barbecue area in the garden. The original ventilation chimney was rescued from the roof of the house to serves as a cowl for outdoor cooking.

Bob McLaren's edict for bathrooms and workrooms is that they should be functional above all else. His design for the bathroom is aggressive and strongly contrasted in colour; a pair of basins against a burnt orange wall stand either side of the oversize bath, while tiles with graduated graphic lines make the room a geometric study in black, white and orange. His workroom is set in a gable end. It has a large contemporary work table by British furniture designer David Field and a mobile trolley/tabouret by Aalvar Aalto for work tools.

The rich master bedroom is a study in grey, beige and burnt orange. Marian Dorn's deep, tufted carpet complements a square, leather, Italian bed covered in heavy fur. A silver-handled, black lacquer chest of drawers by Adnet, a Van der Rohe chair and nesting tables by Mallet-Stevens complete the room.

The winter garden room is stark and cool. Devoted to Aalvar Aalto furniture, no other elements intrude bar a pair of large Kentsia palms. Graphic discipline is carried through to the garden by a flight of steps bordered with evergreen terraces that lead up from the winter garden room to a summer garden carpeted with green lawns. Both these gardens are overlooked by the deck over the winter garden room. Edged with square flower tubs, the balcony space has a simple metal table and French folding chairs painted in clear red – just perfect for alfresco lunches. A Japanese water garden was the inspiration for the front garden, hidden from the street behind a high brick wall. Here we find lily ponds and two tons of carefully selected grey granite stone interspersed with low plant containers.

The master bedroom (facing page) is lit by sloping rooflights covered by grey blinds to mask the harsh top light.

The open-plan living area, seen (left) from the chef's counter top and (above) from the stairs, has furniture placed in parallel curves or lines – another example of McLaren's control in design.

The whole design of this house and garden is disciplined in line and colour, from the horizontal height levels set for the construction work at the start, to the arrangement of furniture and fittings. Even pieces of furniture are placed with parallel partners – the curved chrome seat by Gorska paired with the Rene Herbst dining table is just one example of many such groupings. Colour control in the house continues into the garden. Shades of green are permitted, but other colours are restricted to red and white – white impatiens with red begonias in square tubs, and red garden furniture. Surrounded by grey slabs and grey-green conifers, the carefully trimmed lawns

glow a rich green. This exercise in style was finished by painting bold, red chevrons on the grey front doors and flashing the gates in red – 'to freak out the neighbours' says McLaren.

For a man who has lived in the United States, Holland and France, and who has spent years creating and co-ordinating international advertising campaigns to strict disciplines, designing this house in London was a liberating and rewarding experience. In rescuing the building and creating a living style, McLaren found his metier; this derelict building was the first of many more destined to be re-vitalised by him.

A FEMININE FACELIFT TO STATION PARADE

✧

Two designers were given carte blanche *to convert the corner site of a Victorian parade of houses, called Station Parade, for an owner who had no possessions to be considered in the design. From such an unrestricted brief – the interior designer's near perfect dream – they created a romantically elegant duplex for an owner who had a busy professional and social life and two daughters to accommodate.*

Brick and stone cornices (facing page), decorative ironwork and original Victorian sash windows hide a now feminine interior. Right: the dining room, filled with softened colours and warm light. For an owner who enjoys entertaining, the room has been planned for eight guests to circle a huge, round table. Antique and modern glassware with individual candles provides a glamorous table setting.

Britof the last century has the solid quality of the Victorian era. The corner house of a redbrick terrace in Richmond, complete with the sign 'Station Parade', was bought by Renty Kassam and handed over to two designers as a dreary, brown and black shell of a home.

The rooms, though sombre in tone, had good proportions, but in some areas suffered from insufficient light. The sitting room was painted in dark colours, while the dining room was a dingy place for eating. As a solution, it was decided to remove the dividing wall to make a spacious arch and provide a light and open living space. Elsewhere, the good qualities of the architecture were enhanced. Being on a corner site, the front of the house has a magnificent span of sash windows, three in a wide bay and one on the 'sliced off' corner of the parade, and the rooms are lofty, with good moulding on the ceilings. The designers – Liz van Walsum and Jenny Catling – have made a major feature of both these qualities in the decoration of the two adjoining rooms.

Walls and ceiling painted in warm pink have a deeper shade picking out the ceiling patterns. The windows, painted clean white, have a deep sill that serves as an elegant window seat, while generous Austrian blinds made in glazed cotton allow the daylight to glow through

The emphasis in the sitting room (these pages) centres upon dramatic curtain arrangements and tailored settees. The one painting in the room is of a chair, with a specific accent upon its fabric. Daylight floods the room with gentle pink tones that change at night to richer, warmer tones with the aid of recessed lighting in the moulded ceiling. Feathery bamboo and lilies with gypsophila add to the lightness of the decoration.

the fabric and enrich the room's tone to deep salmon. The curtains of two-tone chevron design in warm pink have been made generously full, but treated as a tailored drape on either side of the wide bay and held by a tie-back of pleated fabric. The stage-like effect is balanced by a deep, frilled valance.

Having made the windows a major feature of the sitting room, the rest of the furnishings are in a restrained, but eminently comfortable, style. Deep sofas, chairs and

upholstered footstools in a neutral, linen colour with a woven diamond design have pleated corners to give a crisp, tailored floor line. Plenty of plain cushions adhere to the uncluttered design, while two octagonal cane tables – one low, the other normal height – have bottom shelves to act as book and magazine racks.

A large modern painting by Jane Patterson of an armchair caught in sunlight fills the entire wall above the white fireplace, and cane baskets with tall feathery bamboo plants maintain the light feeling in the room. By night the room is lit by white bowl spotlights recessed in the ceiling and low table lamps with soft apricot shades, while arrangements of lilies and gypsophila make delicate outlines on the cane tables. Altogether, the room has a strong sense of light, balanced by warm, soft tones.

The main dining room through the wide arch has been designed for effect at night. As the owner enjoys entertaining groups of friends, a large round table has ample room for eight armchairs in cane, all with soft cushions. The table, set with soft peach linen, has tall, individual place candles whose light enhances a mixture of antique and modern glassware, while the centrepiece is a bowl of cream roses and lilies. Large landscape paintings by Anthony Eyton of figures in a misty light fill adjoining corner walls of the dining room. Beautifully lit by ceiling spots to give them a luminous quality, they increase the soft, glamorous atmosphere intended for this end of the room. A small cane corner table, lit by an Art-Deco gilt figure holding a bowl light, adds the final touch to this room's sophistication.

In contrast, the family dining room is attractively relaxed. The buttermilk walls and ceiling are teamed with a deeper tone for cupboards and country chairs. A scrubbed pine table is large enough for dining and preparing food, while a counter-weighted lamp allows for lighting at an adjustable height.

The first floor was given the reverse structural approach. The overlarge main bedroom was divided to provide a bedroom, study and separate master bathroom. The walls and ceiling have been painted a deep rose pink alongside white paintwork and the ceiling mouldings picked out in white and a paler pink. The windows have been treated in a style similar to that of the sitting room, having generous Austrian blinds and full curtains, this time in a large, pink and green floral-printed cotton, but the curtains have been allowed to hang full and drape over the claret carpet.

A pair of cane armchairs with lattice backs and a cane table in the bay window make an inviting breakfast alcove, completed by a drawn threadwork cloth and a jug of scented white lilies. Similarly, the bed has a white Victorian counterpane with piles of drawn threadwork and lace-edged cushions, while clusters of Victorian fluted lamp glasses, suspended by brass chains from the ceiling, fall in groups of three, and the mirror above the bed has a distinctive Victorian *papier mâché* frame. In contrast, the adjoining bathroom has modern lighting, with a battery of tiny spotlights set in the ceiling, so the mirrored bath recess reflects multiple light images.

The building narrows on one wall to form a wedge-shaped room. Whilst this has the advantage of making the room an interesting shape, every inch needed to be utilised to provide enough cupboard space for the owner's daughter. One wall was treated as the sleeping, study and storage space. Floor cupboards have been built under a bunk bed, while the floor-to-ceiling 'headboard' separates the bed from a desk recess and book shelves, which are supported at the other end by a full height wardrobe. Fitting all this along the longer wall of the wedge allows the narrower space to be clear of any obstructions. The shades of blue chosen range from pale delphinium to deep French navy for the carpet and bunk cover. Walls are washed in a tone lighter than the woodwork, which is all coloured blue.

The staircase (facing page) has been treated as a series of linked ante-rooms. A recumbent figure in a painting by Clifford Hall is sympathetic to its stairway position. Below: the blue bedroom, designed to utilise every inch of space in a wedge-shaped area.

Below: a tableau on the first floor landing, formed by a Lloyd Loom chair and a cane table, upon which cream roses stand beside an Art Deco lamp.

On the first landing is found a Lloyd Loom chair beside a cane table spray-painted grey. Overlooked by a pre-Raphaelite painting, the tableau is completed by a bowl of cream roses and an Art-Deco lamp of a figure holding a light. Above the stairs leading to the top floor, a painting by Clifford Hall of a recumbent figure on a stairway is hung beneath a stained glass window, which was installed to give additional light to the newly constructed study. Massive sprays of forsythia arranged in an urn on the floor give a joyous burst of colour to the top landing.

The overall effect offers a pleasing sense of colour, emphasises the importance that lighting can have in changing the decorative mood of a room, and uses day and night lighting to good effect. Having started from scratch, the designers have been able to select specific items to execute their decorative theme. Although plants and cut flowers are used a lot, they are not obtrusive, and, chosen for their delicate outlines and simple arrangements, do not draw attention away from the decorative plan. This interior design by professionals for an owner who has a busy business, social and family life seems to have fulfilled its brief in every respect.

The stairway of the house is more than just a link between floors, as the generously sized landings have been used to create small ante-rooms. The lower wall has a panel of anaglypta which has been retained and painted deep apricot, the walls above are smooth and in a lighter tone. Stair balustrades and doors are painted a rich cream and grey carpets cover the floors.

The breakfast corner in the main bedroom (above and right) might be a stage setting for an elegant play. An antique, drawn-thread cloth, embroidered with butterflies, covers a round table with matching cane armchairs. The vase holding cut Lilium regale is part of a Victorian washstand set. Deep pink for the walls and ceilings is refreshed by the use of crisp white for the ceiling mouldings, window frames and the mantlepiece.

The design for Renty Kassam's bedroom is simply feminine. A white Victorian counterpane covers a bed piled high with lace-edged cushions and lit by clusters of fluted lamp glasses (above). Left: a detail of the fabric combination used for the bedroom curtains and Austrian blinds; large roses in a soft pink and green watered design on the curtains are balanced by plain pink translucent blinds.

VICTORIAN TERRACE TO GLASS PENTHOUSE

*The lofts and attics of a Victorian terrace house in North London
have been gutted to create an imaginative glass penthouse. All hint of
the original nineteenth-century architecture has been removed except for
the framework of the flamboyant turrets, towers and roof. This
skeleton inspired the owners to use the remaining interesting shapes
and angles to form the basis of their modern, clean-lined style.*

Highbury and St Johns Wood in North London are full of tree-lined roads separating terraces of solid, dark red Victorian houses. Eminently respectable and predictable, these residences are graced with wrought-iron railings to the basement service areas, inset front doors with stained glass panels and sombre windows on the ground and first floors that become progressively smaller with ascending floors – the top floors of these houses would have been used for nurseries and living quarters for servants and the rooms would have been smaller in scale. Victorian restraint is eased slightly, however, on a roof of towers, turrets and ornamental stonework.

One such house has had the scale of the attic rooms and the loft reversed. Bought by a surveyor and his wife – who nearly turned away when they saw the overbearing facade – the roof has literally been raised for the creation of an outstanding penthouse, which now offers views all the way to central London. When taking the roof off, the main timber frames were left intact. Then, within this skeleton, a new penthouse was built using the slope of the original roof to make unusually shaped rooms.

A feature of this flat is the large, airy sitting room that opens onto a roof garden. At one side this open-plan room joins a conservatory, and the frame of the original roof gable forms the basis of a massive 'A' fireplace and

Previous pages: (left) a Victorian roof turret, a striking contrast to the modern roof terrace and garden (right).

Clear linear details in the architecture and neutral tones in the furnishings combine to give a sense of spaciousness to the sitting room (right). Italian furniture and a corner wall of books, sculpture and paintings (facing page bottom) are reflected in a glass-topped table (above). The room's neutral tones are relieved by the large leaves of a Kentia palm. A suspended ventilator hood (facing page top), painted in primary colours is a visual division between the clinical kitchen and the dining area.

plant recess. This, in turn, joins the kitchen and dining area, which also has access to the roof garden.

The style of the sitting room is set by its shape. Inspired by the original turret, which once poked through the roof, the room is octagonal, boasting a bay window with strong lines and large glass doors to the garden. All the structural design to the flat is solid and smooth. Windows have thick, square architraves and broad ledges, the starkness of their lines being accentuated by the simple panelling below them. The furnishing of this architectural space is minimal, and beige prevails throughout. A pale stone carpet, diagonally patterned two-tone beige Italian sofas and a simple, leather-covered Eames chair give an uncluttered impression to the room. Curtains fall smooth and straight, without a hint of a flounce, and the Roman blinds are of sand-coloured linen. The modern, steel fireplace hood is surrounded by French floor tiles. The only real splashes of colour here are made by the book collection displayed in a tall, black bookcase and the strong

Above: the low-ceilinged master bedroom, which has been given strength and space by its decoration. Creamy white walls and bed linen combine well with dark antique furniture, the bold outlines of a Moroccan screen and a bookend from San Francisco. The modern interior of the old corner turret provides a smooth ledge (left) for a modern sculpture.

green of Kentsia palms and asparagus ferns, which flourish in a room virtually walled in glass.

The conservatory, walled and roofed in glass, grants one a marvellous feeling of elevation – yet its strong framework gives it a comfortably secure and solid feel. Palms, ferns and a variety of other houseplants grow vigorously here among glass-topped tables and cane chairs.

From this light-filled atmosphere there is a change of key in the combined kitchen and dining room. Here the mood is one of high contrast. Slate-coloured Bulthaup kitchen units are set into an angled bay following the lines of the original pitched roof. A ventilator hood, painted in primary colours, appears as a piece of suspended metal sculpture.

Probably the only hint of Victoriana in the flat is the mirrored chiffonier in rich mahogany at one end of the dining room, which serves to reflect the modern, Italian marble dining table and the grey and steel dining chairs. The visual strength of the long bay window, whose woodwork has been painted black, is not softened by any blinds or curtains – after all, who would wish to blot out such superb tree-top views?

The master bedroom is both high and low key – dark, ornate antiques are set against pale, neutral tones in the carpet and on the walls. The low, sloped ceiling is counterbalanced by a low, wide bed covered in a stone-coloured cotton quilt, whose black headboard was made from a carved Moroccan screen. One of a pair of unusual bookends found in San Fransisco, a black figure with outstretched arms, makes a striking sculpture here amid all the pastel shades.

The penthouse bathroom is fitted with recessed black lacquer Italian units and grill panels of beechwood. A clever use of black heated towel rails, set vertically from floor to ceiling, screen the bidet and lavatory at one end of the bathroom.

Finally, come the fine weather, an additional 'room with a view' is added – the roof garden. Hardwood slats allow any rainwater to be channelled away and the plants are kept in washed shingle. The glass panels below the restraining rail provide protection from the wind and allow the view to remain unobscured for those wishing to recline while sunbathing.

Slate-coloured Bulthaup kitchen units (below) fill an angled bay, following the skeleton lines of the original roof. The window frames are painted black and the windows left bare of curtains or blinds, while pale grey ceramic tiles cover the walls and the floor.

The thickset framework of the conservatory (below) loans a sense of solidity to this roof-top area, while the glass walls and roof provide facetted views of London. The dusk blue light from the sky strengthens the rich colours of the plants.

The dining area (left) mixes a modern Italian marble-topped table and grey and steel dining chairs with the only piece of Victoriana left in the conversion – a rich mahogany chiffonier, fronted and topped with mirrors and marble.

THE RESTORATION OF A TUDOR MANOR HOUSE

⟡

This home has been restored by Mrs Jacqueline Thwaites, Principal of the Inchbald School of Design in London and author of numerous books and articles on design and decoration. The school aims to give students a disciplined approach to interior design based on a sound knowledge of the history of design, and stresses the need for preservation of buildings and artefacts of previous generations. For this reason, the restoration of the garden and interior of the manor house at Ayot St Lawrence is of particular interest.

The Queen Anne wing (facing page) looks onto a terrace laid in brick and flagstones with secluded corners shielded by shrubs. Above: a pedestal urn planted with sedum.

The Manor House at Ayot St Lawrence was built in 1536 for Nicholas Bristowe, Keeper of the Queen's Jewels. It the years that followed, it slid gently down the social scale from this connection with Henry VIII to become a dower house, then a farmhouse and ultimately a farm worker's semi-detached cottage. It was finally left empty, with only the surrounding country claiming ownership over the once-elegant gardens.

When Brigadier and Mrs Thwaites found the property some twelve years ago, it had been neglected since the Thirties, yet it still possessed the original dignity of a house of style. The front of the house of narrow, red Tudor bricks and stone-mullioned windows has an additional elevation built in 1715. As Mrs Jacqueline Thwaites is a firm believer in basing contemporary design on the skills and achievement of earlier craftsmen, this manor house presented her with a golden opportunity to practise her basic philosophy that the history of

Light from the staircase window (above) streams through a collection of nineteenth-century vaseline glass.

The white-painted ceiling of the dark, oak-panelled dining room (right) reflects daylight back onto the light mahogany table and Hepplewhite chairs. Turquoise glazed cotton, with an oriental design of fruit and flowers in warm peach and brown, frames the windows.

Below: the table setting. The travelling lamps contain a device with which to push candles up as they burn down, and the silk pleated shades can be folded away in their travelling case.

architecture and design must provide the basis for interior work.

The owners have a great love of flowers and, as restoring gardens takes almost longer than restoring houses, they planned for the future in laying down a formal knot garden in front of the Tudor wing, with dwarf box hedges and green lawn squares interspersed with shingle and formal flower gardens. This is in the style of gardens which originated in 1494 and which were popular in the sixteenth and seventeenth centuries. Beds and low-growing plants, such as clipped lavender and box, were laid out in a formal pattern that sometimes resembled a maze or a large knot of rope. As bedding plants were unknown in Tudor times, inert materials such as coloured sands, chalk, and even coal, were used to make patterns and give gardens a permanent decorative feature. The more intricate gardens resemble embroidery when viewed from terraces and balconies, and indeed, the Tudor window of the Manor House, which spans the floor-to-ceiling height of the first floor, gives an elevated view of the Thwaites' knot garden as you ascend the central staircase.

The rest of the garden wilderness was reclaimed to make sheltered walled gardens to protect an outdoor swimming pool, while terraces were laid in brick and secluded by banks of hebe and potentilla shrubs to form

Mrs Thwaites replaced the brick mantlepiece in the dining room (left) with a dark oak one to match the panelling. The gouache of Lake Geneva hung above it was brought back from Switzerland by Dr. Thomas Arnold, the famous head of Rugby School, and has been handed down through the family. Flowers gathered from the garden make a summer froth of scabious, gypsophila and buddleia in the fireplace.

dictates the furniture, which centres round the welcoming log fire.

Individual groupings of furniture and objects create separate vignettes of style. An Edwardian portrait of a lady in black is placed near a stand of specimen glasses filled with mauve scabious. Yellow antirrhinum mixed with Mountbatten roses and golden *Alchemilla mollis* make a glowing bowl of flowers on the warm-toned octagonal table. Another table was stripped of black varnish to reveal its light oak grain and grouped with square, eighteenth-century decanters and a single spray of white lilies in an alabaster vase.

Oak panelling in the dining room made it a sombre place for meals. Its overbearing quality has been lightened by painting the ceiling white to reflect light back onto the mahogany table and Hepplewhite chairs. The scale of the room demanded a fireplace with dignity, so Mrs Thwaites replaced the existing brick surround with an oak mantel, elaborately carved with lions' heads,

quiet corners in which to enjoy lunch during the English summer. The rest was laid to lawn to complement the grandeur of an existing cedar and other mature trees.

Turning to the interior, the temptation to use simpler modern treatments was avoided, and Mrs Thwaites created a home in the mellow English country tradition. Each room is treated individually, though throughout there is a recurring decorative theme connected with the Thwaites' love of flowers, first in the furnishings and then in the various ebullient bowls of cut blooms from the garden, each one carefully chosen to echo the decorative style of the room in which it stands.

The Oriental influence in Queen Anne houses sparked off the choice of fabrics – cream glazed cotton with Japanese blossoms – in the drawing room. Walls flushed with pale peach give a sympathetic glow to the dark wooden beams and, although elegance is the key, comfort

cherubs and acanthus leaves. In summer the fireplace is filled with flowers, such as blue-toned scabious, buddleia and agapanthus clouded with gypsophila.

Rather than obscure the view from the leaded windows of the oak staircase with drapes, glass shelves have been fitted to increase the display area for a large collection of nineteenth-century glass. In such a perfect setting, the glass glows with this natural backlighting.

The generous height of the first floor allows for rooms on the grand scale. The master bedroom, in tones of cream and pink, has a lace-covered bed and a glazed cotton bed canopy dominating one end, an elegant nineteenth-century day bed the other. Another floral echo of pink roses mixed with freesia and santolina highlight the Japanese chest and give a quiet colour key to the room.

Other bedrooms have the same elegant yet comfortable style, with varying emphasis on colour. In one instance,

The bedroom's geometric blue and white cotton curtains (above) are matched with a blue and green poppy design for the upholstered blanket chest and bedhead.

Above: an arrangement of freesias and cream and blush roses on a Japanese vellum chest displays an exact eye for colour. The main bedroom (right) is a blend of creams and softly tinged roses. Matching flower printed glazed cotton for the bed hangings and upholstery blends beautifully with the Japanese chest and flowers. The dressing table is curtained in cream silk and a heavily fringed cream lace coverlet graces the bed.

blue and white glazed cotton makes a cool room, the spotted white muslin bed canopy held by a gilt ceiling crown. A lace-covered table has a carved wooden mirror that reflects a collection of silver-topped glass toilet bottles and a glass bowl of deep blue irises. The Oriental influence is repeated in another bedroom, where a collection of Japanese blossom pictures in soft greens and pinks is displayed. Cotton satin quilts in pearl pink are colour-linked to a Victorian flowered chintz for the headboards and curtains.

The finished result has great elegance in its delicate, underlying appreciation of colour that has been carried through in exact details. Flower designs, which play a key role in the choice of textiles, are repeated in freshly gathered blossoms from the garden. A simple bowl of white sweet peas tinged with a few pink stems echoes the tones of the master bedroom, while a rose-printed

A comfortable study bedroom (below) displays the quiet dignity typical of English country life. A silver-framed photograph of the owners with their labrador dog and an ancient Teddy Bear propped against the table lamp give a personal touch to this book-lined retreat.

Right: a corner of the main bedroom, where a silk pleated fan in a frame complements the colours of the dressing table.

blind has matching apricot-coloured full blown roses in a cut glass vase placed nearby that are so similar they could have been used for the artist's reference.

This is a house where, if the walls could talk, there would be many tales to tell of the different lifestyles of its successive owners. Yet for the present, its twentieth-century owners have given splendour back to the Manor House by combining elegance and comfort for stylish, modern-day country living.

Above: one of a pair of nineteenth-century sewing tables that graces the drawing room (left). Inlaid with satinwood and holly, they double as a games tables.

Queen Anne and French Fashion

◇

The Old Mansion is a seventeenth-century Queen Anne residence in London possessing great architectural style. As the family home of fashion designer Nicole Farhi, it is evidence that her creativity is not limited to fashion alone. Original, zestful designs, unhampered by convention, capitalise on the space created over three hundred years ago.

Decorative ironwork built onto curved piers forms a raised verandah (left) that stretches the width of this Queen Anne house. Vines flourish in the adjacent conservatory wing (above).

For this house owner, brilliance in design is not limited to one sphere, though time is a curbing factor. Nicole Farhi, who is the French talent behind the clothes bearing the French Connection label, spends her time between designing for this mass market and creating collections for her own shops. Quarterly trips to India and Hong Kong and a working life in both Paris and London leave her little breathing space for planning a personal lifestyle. Because of this, the house's interior design is not being precisely planned, but arrives in bursts of inspiration. Convention does not inhibit her style, so the rooms which have been completed have a refreshing disregard for cohesion or period.

The grace of the seventeenth-century entrance hall is left to speak for itself. Having a massive, white, panelled door, wall panelling simply treated and enough space for large, black and white floor tiles, Nicole Farhi's design assurance leaves it starkly clear of possessions.

The sitting room is of an equally imposing size, graced with a series of floor-to-ceiling windows and a wide archway through to an adjoining room. Everything is painted white, but there is a rich cinnamon brown carpet. A pair of giant sofas, built to her design, are covered in a textured fabric of visionary white brought back from

India, while curtains of chevron stripes are in a blend of cream, through orange, to soft red and maroon.

Low, green tables made from antique Indian doors with glass tops match the scale of the sofas. Baskets containing large bowls of orchids and lilies placed on these tables are set off by a reclining bronze statue by David Backhouse. These baskets are unusual, being fashioned from vines grown in arid areas of France and Italy that have been trained in coils to withstand the wind and protect the grapes. When the branches of the vines are pruned and entwined they form attractive basket shapes.

This room of suitably large-scale furniture has two equally important pictures at either end. An unframed oil painting by Harry Watson of diners in a restaurant overlooking Lake Garda is a frozen image in time, while the other canvas is a riot of energy, an impression of the French cabaret star Mistinguette at Le Bal de Marine, depicting French sailors and dancing girls in constant

Classically simple textures of wood and stone (below) set the style for the dining room. The lines of the rectangular wall panelling are repeated in a massive stone table, while the curved lines of the recessed glass cupboards are followed by the black Thonet dining chairs and central Napoleon III billiard lamp.

Relaxed entertaining centres upon a marble-topped bar (facing page) transported from Paris. The warm tones of this Bakelite and chrome bar blend with a rich red Indian carpet and rattan furniture. A bronze figure and car model complete the 'Thirties influence.

The colours in an animated picture of the French caberat star Mistinguette (above) harmonize with those of the Indian cushions on a cane and bamboo settee in the sitting room.

Antique Indian doors, protected by glass, make unusual low tables in the White Room (right), where delicate Michaelmas daisies, orchids and lilies fill a basket of twisted vines placed beside a David Backhouse bronze.

movement. A bamboo and cane three-seater sofa and three Indian cushions accompany this picture.

Nicole Farhi enjoys the company of friends and her informal entertaining centres around 'The Bar', which was rescued from her favourite café when Les Halles was closed in Paris. It is a classic reminder of the Thirties in Bakelite, marble and chrome. The owners not only agreed to sell it to their regular customer, they also transported and erected it in the room adjoining the White Room. Rattan furniture and a rich Indian carpet of strong reds completes the dash element of the room, all of which stands in total contrast to the cool sitting room seen through the archway.

Above: the view across 'The Bar' to the seating area in the Thirties living room. The archway leads through to the formal White Room (right).

Her individual style shines through in the dining room. Centuries of paint have been stripped from the mellow wood panels covering the walls, the recesses either side of the marble fireplace have been painted black, and glass shelves are used to make open glass cabinets. These tie in with the black Thonet bentwood chairs, whose delicate tracery makes the table designed by Nicole Farhi even more impressive. A massive stone slab, so heavy that it took seven men to carry it into the house (amidst doubts that the floors would sustain the weight) is a designer's dream. Its porosity was overcome by daily waxing for two whole months. When this series of pictures was taken it was laid with black mats and white porcelain, but this is alternated with old French damask cloths and silver Victorian cutlery. Eighteenth-century landscapes and a Napoleon III billiard lamp with blue shades complete this stylish room.

White panelled walls and a white, Brussels-weave carpet make another open canvas for Nicole Fahri's design ideas in the main bedroom. Every conceivable shade of brown in patterned and plain velvet makes an enormous patchwork quilt for the bed, which stands on a wooden dais. The Eastern influence in furniture and objects – particularly the rich sheen of Persian silk rugs

and painted Indian hangings – adds to the rich tones in this all-white space. A nineteenth-century Chinese paper lantern, another find from Paris, lights the room.

The complex architectural shapes of the attic floor make almost sculptural designs now it has been painted pure white, while a particularly low ceiling profile is etched in black for both practical and aesthetic reasons. Nicole Fahri's design for living is sparse, but her talent for tailoring for functional modern life is evidently unlimited. A fireplace that makes an excellent bookcase in the study is a perfect example of this.

Finally, the London garden is enclosed by a conservatory with vines and a delicate, raised verandah, which is partly glazed, partly open to enjoy the grace of this Queen Anne manor house. Throughout, it is clear that the elegant space offered by the seventeenth-century building has not interfered with Nicole Fahri's individualistic approach to living in style.

Above left: part of the elevated verandah, glazed and enclosed to make a conservatory living room and furnished with cane and India rugs.

A tracery of ironwork (above) makes a delicate frame for an enclosed garden filled with roses and lavender.

GREENHOUSE FOLLY IN THE SKY

Eccentricity in the nineteenth century in building a rooftop greenhouse to nurture orchids allowed a twentieth-century designer the opportunity to create a rooftop living space in line style.

The creative director of an international advertising agency, Bob McLaren spends his leisure hours creating modern living space in old buildings, particularly those dating from the turn of the century. He retains all original features which he feels have architectural integrity, and guts the rest.

This unique enclave of north London studios was constructed between 1878 and 1884 by Sir Thomas B. Beckett. What made the last two units – Numbers 3 and 3A – irresistible to Bob McLaren was the nineteenth-century folly built on top of the two-storey building – a huge greenhouse spanning the roof, complete with heating system, drains and even a fireplace. The greenhouse, the real reason for buying the whole house, has been turned from the folly of some nineteenth-century gent with a passion for growing orchids, into a folly of a twentieth-century designer with a passion for crystal clear lines. In rescuing and modernising the structure, Bob MacLaren has preserved it for another decade.

The dominant shape in this living space (right) is pyramidal and the assertive colour is red. A ladder stair leads to a suspended sleeping area above the dining room and kitchen.

Facing page: the exterior of the studio buildings, built in the late nineteenth century. The removal of a chimney breast enabled a glass-walled kitchen to be projected beyond the studio room, while industrial cladding makes a functional access to the balcony sleeping area (right).

Partnered with grey relief, the red colour key of McLaren's design for the interior changes the character of the original doorway (above).

Having acquired No. 3 and 3A, he embarked on what he describes as a schizophrenic exercise in design. The bottom half he designed as clean-classical, conservative chic. The clean-classical look was achieved by using two tones of grey throughout but reversing the standard scheme – all woodwork dark and all walls light. The use of dusty rose accents in carpeting and walls in bedrooms injected the conservative chic. Streamlined bathrooms fitted with vast round tubs were treated in a cool white style, with brilliant white tiled floors and walls flashed with yellow stripes. The bathspace is a tribute to modern technology, epitomised by stark but functional Zenda heated towel rails and a huge ep-

Above: Bob McLaren believes in finite and fun design, and his own is colour related.

Above: his fun element – an ancient friend, seated on a stool, watches passers-by.

oxy resin bath from Bigger Splash, but it is also a homage to Mondrian, whose style McLaren uses freely in tiles surrounding the shower and mirror.

A massive chimney breast that ran the entire height of the building was removed to enable McLaren to construct a lofty, thirty-foot-long kitchen overlooking the walled garden. Reminiscent of a greenhouse, it is mostly brilliant white, highlighted by flashes of yellow. Basic units bought from Habitat have been refined by David Field to provide maximum efficiency in minimum space, and keyed with primary yellow and red for tiles and work surfaces. But to get back to the greenhouse in the sky, the raison d'etre for the whole project.

Here a battered and very exposed roof has been transformed into an elegant rooftop dining space, which has been extended to the end of the building by the simple device of duplicating the original windows of the old greenhouse and glazing the roof to create a greenhouse in

Right: red and grey units, flashed with brilliant yellow, make a highly efficient, minimal-space kitchen.

miniature. Painted charcoal grey, with yellow lines, and
with the windows shielded by fine, grey, metallic blinds,
it forms a stark setting for the lacquer-and-chrome Art
Deco table by René Herbst and Gae Aulentis Solus
chairs. The cast-iron Victorian columns and steel supports for the roof of the original greenhouse have been
retained and painted matt red to contrast with the grey
panels and darker grey glazing bars of the roof. All sloping
areas of the roof are clad in lightweight industrial roofing
and McLaren has retained the vertical glass fenestration,
only replacing the original glass with double glazing.

A vast see-through living area has infinitely controll-
able light with walls of glass that turn to smooth steel at
night. The sleepspace, built as an open gallery at one
end, is fitted with red and grey furniture designed in
conjunction with David Field. The gallery is reached by
means of an industrial steel stairway rising from the centre of the living space.

With the final touch of removing all the doors
(McLaren regards these as impediments), this residence
is now a far cry from the nineteenth-century glass house
built for nurturing orchids, standing instead as a modern
concept in linear design which McLaren perfects in all
his buildings.

Throughout this former greenhouse, daylight is filtered through metallic blinds (these pages) which turn to smooth steel surfaces when closed at night.

The opulence of the Roman-style tiled 'pool' in the bathroom (left) is enhanced by mirrored walls that present multiple images of the blue and white design.

Mason ironware plates laid on a heavy lace cloth (overleaf left) create a distinctive setting in the dining room. The lofty, narrow sitting room (overleaf right) demanded furniture scaled to match the space. Silk festoon curtains on the French windows block the harsher daylight.

THE MIGRANT DESIGNER

◆

Those who buy property from Mimi O'Connell have all the traumas of moving home ironed out. She does not regard herself as a true professional interior designer as she styles for her own occupation, rather than that of the final owners. Her style is clean and uncluttered, the emphasis on elegant, well-run establishments that have an overtone of opulence. Another chapter shows a trompe l'oeil *basement flat designed by her, while this is the 1982 O'Connell version of a terraced house in Belgravia, just awaiting her departure.*

Mimi O'Connell had a roving childhood, which probably whetted her insatiable appetite for moving. She was born in Italy, grew up in Argentina and Brazil, married an American and travels on a Swiss passport. She has rarely lived in one place for longer than two years, and she makes a business of buying houses and apartments, decorating and living in them for a brief period to iron out the organisation problems of a home, and then selling them to move on to another challenge. Packing cases do not daunt her, as they herald the excitement of another decorating exercise.

She has a reputation for decorating at great speed, although the finished result does not appear hurried. She refuses to fuss about waiting for items which are difficult to obtain, instead concentrating upon materials which are immediately available to give the whole operation a definite vigour.

Her approach is always organised – sound and light installation comes before decorating so that all the mechanics can be well hidden – and her style changes from the starkly architectural in large spaces, to utilising

more conventionally decorative objects for limited floor areas. Comfort and style govern her designs. Bathrooms are seen as extensions of dressing rooms, and have over-generous supplies of linen, living rooms are designed for party gatherings in comfort, and dining rooms are for quiet appreciation of good food in a gentle light. She rarely departs from a basic light-wall approach, though she admits to an itch to design an all-red room.

The initial problems with this property were its rooms which, though they were generously proportioned in their height, had limited floor space and were harshly lit through the French windows. These she softened with silk festoon curtains, so removing the glare, and this is particularly successful in the sitting room, which is narrow, long and runs the full depth of the house. Objects have been chosen in scale with the height of the room, and furniture placed as solid 'islands' to leave the maximum floor space free. Neutral, off-white walls and deep cream festoon blinds leave the furnishing to set the

decorative style. Green Fortuny fabric covers a pair of banquettes set in the middle of the room and, for continuity, the same design in gold has been used for the generous table cover. The magnificent painting of a trumpet lily by Johann Labriolla hangs above a pair of natural linen-covered sofas and, positioned immediately opposite the ornate gilt mirror above the fireplace, this picture is of prime importance. The other end of the room has a raised banquette covered in beige and white mattress ticking. Surrounded by bookshelves, this forms a corner for solitary reading, or else additional seating for a gathering.

Blue and white cotton ticking covers the walls of the dining room, and is echoed in the festoon curtains. The blue theme was dictated by a collection of Mason ironware plates, which look impressive on a lace-covered table lit by indigo candles in silver holders. The two bedrooms also follow the blue and white pattern, where swathes of simple fabrics have been used generously.

Mimi O'Connell admits her obsession with generosity may have run away with her in the bathroom. The Roman-style tiled pool does allow the occupant total submersion, while the surrounding mirror panels increase the illusion of size still further.

The purchasers of Mimi O'Connell homes have a head start for the smoothest move ever. She sometimes chooses to make a clean sweep of her possessions and has been known to sell the house with all the contents. On one occasion, as Mimi O'Connell left with just suitcases, the new owner was able to give a dinner party in her beautifully appointed establishment that very same night!

The master bedroom (below) holds an impressive, eighteenth-century Venetian bed swathed in finely printed blue and white cotton. Mimi O'Connell's flowers are simply arranged, yet always large in scale or quantity. Either in paintings or in reality, lilies fill this Belgravia home.

DINING-AT-HOME STYLE

The English Garden Restaurant in Lincoln Street, London, was designed to create an atmosphere of dining at someone's luxuriously appointed home. The decoration was planned for customers to enjoy the ambience, and as Michael Smith once said 'the food is just a bonus'. The idea was to create ebullient, gracious settings as far removed from a conventional restaurant as possible. Though it may seem odd to include a restaurant in such a book as this, the aim of Michael Smith and Malcolm Livingstone in starting the venture was not how many customers could be accommodated, but how to create the look of dining at home.

Facing page: Malcolm Livingstone's English Garden Restaurant. The dining room on the ground floor (right) provides an ebullient contrast to the cool exterior.

Although designed for restaurant dining, the style here points to ways conservatories (right) can be used for entertaining at home. The coolness of white – the right background for plants – is coloured by the choice of a warm pink damask for the table linen. Concentrating the introduction of colour in the table settings allows infinite changes within a neutral background.

The marbled effect in the narrow hallway (far right) was achieved by applying well-soaked wallpaper of a broken grey and white design over every surface and protrusion to form a smooth textured plane. Woodwork marbled with grey paint adds to this effective treatment.

If it were to be used as a restaurant, the long, narrow hall, with its excessively high ceilings, would need to take the passage of a large number of people. Michael Smith was told that papering over the cornices would be too difficult but, in fact, by choosing a broken grey and white design – rather like screwed up newsprint – on a heavyweight paper, he was able to have this applied, well soaked, to mould over the ceiling, walls, cornices and anything else that protruded. The really wet paper acted like *papier mâché* and sculpted the narrow vault into a cohesive grey and white space, while the double glass-panelled doors with Gothic tracery are given a grey marbling effect to tie in with the walls. Only the addition of a narrow marble table, a red-framed Picasso print of flowers, and two red lamps were needed to create a practical, yet elegant, entrance.

Michael Smith grew up among textiles. His family was in the weaving and dyeing business, so he learnt the art of moulding fabrics to suit designs and the basic behaviour of different yarns early in life. He chose all natural yarns for the fabrics as they stand up to rougher treatment. Curtains were considered to be an important part of the decor, so their designs were tucked and pinned by Michael himself, and then handed over to Whitby Oliver in Yorkshire to finish.

First the ceiling and mouldings were papered in a warm pink tone from Osborne and Little (again using the wet paper technique to cover the cornice shapes), and then the walls were lined in plastic down to the chair rail. Two-tone matching cotton fabric was finely pleated to cover the walls, which is not as impractical as it sounds because the walls can be sponged down with water.

A broken-toned pink wallpaper and matching cotton fabric provide a rich background to the sitting room (far left). Keeping within the same colour range, a variety of velvet, damask and grosgrain adds to the opulence.

An unusual version of a Tudor doublet inspired the folded curtains (above and left), lined in a plain tone. This room is a fine example of the art of blending fabrics to achieve a decorative impact.

The sleeve detail on a Tudor doublet inspired the theatrical curtains. Made flat and lined in a lighter tone, the curtains were battened onto a board, then folded back in a large diagonal pleat. The 'slash' of a Tudor costume was made as an inverted pleat down the edge and the ruched lining fabric held by a series of bows. A private dining room uses the same basic scheme, but in tones of beige and apricot.

The 'cumulus cloud' grey and white paper used in the hall papers all the architectural details in the restaurant dining room, with the fireplace and chair rail marbled in a darker grey. The entire width of the room is taken over by flamboyant curtains. Set back from the window on a massive curtain rod, plain white muslin is edged with an 'over-the-top' print of giant blue, green, pink and orange flowers, tied back and held by brass knobs.

These vibrant designs have an irreverent attitude to taste, but manage to achieve a lavish atmosphere without excessive expenditure. Michael Smith's ebullient approach will be sadly missed on the London scene, but his creativity in English cooking will live on through the many books he wrote during his lifetime.

A private dining room (below) uses another basic scheme of colour tones, but without the added influence of pattern or texture. Soft apricot for the walls above the chair rail deepens to a beige with a hint of sage for the lower wall, complemented by quietly draped curtains. Branched candelabras and mahogany furniture complete a rich but tranquil room.

Above: a red-framed Picasso flower painting hangs beside red candle lamps and a bowl of polyanthus to form a compact still life on a marble table. The flamboyant use of printed fabric is tempered with plain tones to make a theatrical setting for dining beside a large window (facing page).

A CAMOUFLAGED APARTMENT IN KNIGHTSBRIDGE

✧

Starting from scratch is not the only way to deal with the unwelcome fittings of a residence's previous occupants. An owner of a Knightsbridge apartment called in designer Diana Phipps to sort out his problems, and she has solved them with the inventive use of fabric and paint to camouflage offensive joinery. This solution saves the time involved in dismantling and then rebuilding, and also halves the costs.

Indian cotton in Rasta-coloured stripes of coral green and gold covers all the upper walls and cupboard doors in the living room (left). The large bay window gives space for a modern Korean desk and a group of Yucca trees. The star-patterned block floor was restored after years under carpeting, while the coffee table was a standard kitchen table before Mrs Phipps cut off the legs and stippled it with oil paints to repeat the bamboo effect of the wall panelling.

P ossession of a new home can trigger a great urge to alter and change what the previous owners installed. When the new owner took over this apartment in Knightsbridge, a host of hideous plywood closets reaching to the ceiling were a daunting prospect. Whilst they provided useful storage, they were visually impossible to tolerate. Diana Phipps was called in to see what could be done to sort out the problems. With an imaginative, rather than destructive, eye she kept nearly all the previous owners' fittings, and yet gave the flat a cohesive design.

The spacious living room had obviously once been the main living room of a Victorian home, while the kitchen, bathroom, long, narrow hall and an odd-shaped extra room had since been squeezed into the space where the original staircase stood. The new owner had no furniture, only three favourite Balinese batiks, which were to be included in the design. The brief given to Mrs Phipps was to start from this limited base, so the atmosphere of the apartment would clearly have to be tropical.

A 'Batak' batik (right), stretched as a wall hanging and framed with large bamboo poles, was the starting point for the theme of the living room. The generous sofa, designed by Diana Phipps, gives ample seating and room for sleep, and also hides a built-in sound system. Diminishing corner shelves make pyramid cupboards in the wall recesses.

She chose 'Batak' batik – a scene depicting a Javanese rhinoceros, tropical palms and a snow-clad mountain – for a wall hanging in the living room, using the muted vegetable dye shades to set the colour key for the rest of the room. Another vegetable-dyed fabric, this time from India in Rasta-coloured stripes of coral, green and gold, covers all the walls. Thin bamboo strips finish where the fabric joins the original moulded ceiling. The dado, the panelled doors and the window surround have been hand stippled with oil paints to give a bamboo effect.

Rather than fit standard corner shelves and cupboards, which would be overwhelmingly tall in such a small space, Mrs Phipps has built sets of diminishing shelves, edged and framed with bamboo, to give a pyramid corner shape on either side of the bay window. The original, elegantly star-patterned parquet floor, discovered under layers of wall-to-wall carpeting, has been highly polished and left uncovered. With the help of a carpenter, Diana Phipps designed a large sofa bed eleven feet long with a bamboo base and ends. A shelf behind this conceals all the sound equipment, while the speakers are in the base of the sofa, leaving narrow gaps in the bamboo facing for the sound to escape.

The kitchen was a narrow, high room, well equipped with a ghastly medley of cupboards and shelves. Should everything be ripped out and then replaced involving double expense and upheaval? It still would not have solved the impossible proportions of the room, so Mrs

Phipps decided that everything should be left alone, and called in the painter Christopher Bentley to camouflage the whole room with a jungle mural. Ceiling, walls, cupboards and shelves disappeared under green foliage and animals.

The bedroom was another mass of plywood closets, obviously used to house the vast wardrobe of the previous occupant. Again imaginative, rather than destructive, design decided that they should be kept and covered with fabric so that only the hinges show. Two of the doors were removed so that a mahogany tallboy could be set flush into part of the cupboard space.

The last room of the flat, which serves as an intimate dining space, a spare room or an overflow area, was probably part of the staircase of the original house, having an unbelievably high and narrow window echoing the strange proportions of the room. The ceiling has now been tented irregularly with coral cotton fabric draped over bamboo, and a plastic fan, grained by Diana Phipps to appear wooden, has been placed in the centre of the ceiling to add to the tropical feel. The coral fabric also camouflages the walls and still more plywood cupboards, where, with a Phipps flash of genius, carved doors taken from a broken old Armoire have been inserted.

With the rising cost of manpower and materials, an imaginative approach to interior design can often overcome financial strictures, as demonstrated in this seemingly hopeless case.

Above: the view through the doorway to the kitchen reveals the jungle mural of Christopher Bentley. Left: the 'extra' room of the flat, which doubles as an intimate dining space and a spare room. The high, irregularly shaped space – once part of an original staircase – has been tented with a coral cotton fabric, which also covers the walls and the plywood cupboards. Carved doors from an old armoire turn inelegant storage into a design feature.

The bedroom walls were a mass of plywood closets that provided extensive storage but looked ugly. By carefully covering all the doors and surrounds with batik fabric so only the hinges were visible, and by removing two doors so that a mahogany tallboy (right) could be set flush against the wall, a total transformation is achieved without losing valuable space. A collection of English futurist prints of the 'Twenties adds to the cupboards' concealment, while rush chairs painted black by Diana Phipps complete the now elegant room.

The navy Javanese batik print in the bedroom (left) has been meticulously pleated to form a central tent over the bed. This steel four-poster was once rusty and had to be sandblasted to its present gleaming elegance. Tucked plain cotton hangings set off the intricate metal bedhead, while another rich batik covers the bed in deep reds and grey blues. The mirror was made from a broken Indian screen and reflects a collection of Jamaican Rastafarian animals. The oriental carpet bordered in blue completes the colour theme. With rising costs this lateral thinking in design makes sense.

WILLOW HOUSE IN CHESHIRE

This Edwardian house in Cheshire – formerly a girls' school – took one year to convert and decorate. With three living rooms, a pair of bathrooms and five bedrooms (more rooms than the average family might wish to tackle), the style was to be simple but effective – an object lesson in positive thinking in the use of colour. Making the most of architectural details and room proportions with effective but economic schemes, the owners have created a relaxed and welcoming family home.

Willow House is a square, symmetrical building, with a central gable over a pair of arches, one of which frames the recessed front door while the other surrounds a tall sash window above it. The roof's elaborately detailed cornice is painted white, in striking contrast to the house's dark brick facade.

With rooms well-lit and generously proportioned, not much structural alteration was required to create style at Willow House. Structural work was needed, though, to repair the roof, gutters, chimneys and flooring before decoration could begin. One of the advantages of having an over-abundance of rooms is that there is space in which to live unhindered by conversion work and this was part of the owners' plan. In all, it took six months to complete the structural work and another next six months to decorate and furnish the house – just a year from start to finish.

Two of the living rooms were knocked into one to make a large and elegant lounge. With walls bathed in warm peach, and a carpet cleverly matched to their stippled tones, the overall effect in this room is cooled by the choice of fabric – a white glazed cotton patterned by

At night, Willow House's windows and doors show in white relief against its dark brick exterior (facing page).

Above: a collection of English blue porcelain plates hang on clear yellow walls.

larger-than-life peach flowers and broad green leaves – for
the modern sofa, armchairs and the curtains. The wide
bay windows suit an elegantly swathed valance, while self
fabric tie-backs prevent the curtains from cutting daylight
and obscuring the panelled shutters of the sash windows.
A willow green rug and a soft blue fabric on the antique
chaise longue and chair link the threads of this colour
scheme. During the summer, the pine and marble fireplace becomes a fine display area for houseplants, which
are all grouped together within the fender rail, whilst
throughout the year flowers are arranged beside the table
lamps, to be caught in pools of light in the evening.

The family living room is an equally cheerful mixture
of buttercup and blue, enhanced by the original fireplace's conversion into a raised open fire. A small broken
print fabric for the Chesterfield sofa and antique chair
repeats the wallpaper pattern, while a mahogany music
stand hints at the room's use for family music-making.

Though wishing to retain the period qualities of the
house elsewhere, the owners intended the kitchen to be
as modern and as streamlined as possible, geared to the
demands of family life. Crisp white units with pine green
trim make for a strictly functional cooking area, while
pinstriped wallpaper in green and white covers the walls,

An arrangement of furniture in front of an arched sash window on the landing (right) is typical of the owner's decorative flair. Deep blue curtains printed with red poppies follow the curve of the window, a curve repeated in the shelf alcove (below) at the top of the stairs.

and pine green paint outlines the windows, skirtings and door surrounds. A green-stained table and folding café seats make graphic shapes on the white tiled floor, and the windows are left uncluttered by blinds or curtains, the sill used for a collection of herb pots. In all, a smart decorative effect is achieved at minimum cost.

On the first floor, imaginative treatment of the arched sash window on the landing has turned a narrow, tunnel-like space into a decorative triumph. Butter yellow gloss on the walls contrasts with curtains of red flowers on a deep blue ground which are draped back with self pat-

terned tie-backs to follow the curve of the window. A pair of balloon-back chairs, upholstered in the same fabric, and a small, octagonal table complete the tableau. The lovely shape of the curved window is echoed at the top of the stairs by an alcove displaying blue and white china.

Pine furniture with terracotta and white wallpaper and a self-tone carpet make an attractive and practical colour scheme for the children's bedrooms, while the scale of the main bedroom encourages more ambitious designs. Grey and peach flower-patterned wallpaper has been used for the walls above the dado, with a linked fabric design for

Children's bedrooms dictate practical colours for youthful behaviour. The choice of warm terracotta (left) makes a subtle partner for pine furniture and will not inhibit relaxed enjoyment.

A bamboo and cane side table acts as a toiletry top in the bathroom (right). Green trim in the all-white kitchen (below) makes for a smart eating recess, where pinstriped wallpaper and green-stained woodwork combine to form an effective decor at minimum cost.

Away from the dining recess, the kitchen (facing page) is clinically streamlined. Here the space has been organised for practical family life, having an all-white floor and units detailed in pine green. Nothing has been allowed to break either the uncluttered lines or the simple colour scheme of green and white.

the curtains and bed furnishings. The wall below the white dado has been left in a plain tone and a printed border made to accent the wall division and ceiling moulding. The curtain drapes to the bed are lined in slate grey and held by brass rosettes, while the gathered fabric valance on the sash windows is finished with grey bows. Blue agapanthus blooms with broad leaves in a glass jug placed beside a grey-shaded bed lamp completes this delicate colour scheme.

No attempt was made to modernise the charm of the original bathroom. The claw-legged bath is painted the same colour as the stippled cream walls of anaglypta paper, while the deep window sills have become indoor 'window boxes' for trailing houseplants. A bamboo and cane table for towels and a bowl of white gypsophila add to the period style.

The knowledge to start this house from scratch was gleaned from making eight moves in twelve years – not everyone's preferred way of gaining design experience. But it has paid off – a practical approach using simple schemes to make the most of the house's architectural details has produced an extremely attractive home. In fact, the success of Willow House encouraged Suzie Casson to open a design workshop in Manchester, and she is now helping others make equally beautiful moves.

The basic two-up, two-down exterior of this 1820s house (right) was left intact in the conversion and some of the original details remain in the decorative brickwork above the plastered lower half of the building. Rusticated keystones (below) and inset panels to the recessed front door have been edged in white against a sand-coloured exterior. Decorative tiles cover the entrance steps, while the elaborate railings have been replaced by some of angular steel.

GOTHIC THEME WITH GLASS

Conventional shapes in houses need not inhibit an expansion in living style. This 1820s house in London has not been extended, yet an ingenious concept to replace bricks and slates with glass has totally altered the character of the interior. The decorating design owes much to the ability of the owner to appreciate unusual furniture and to recognise its potential. Behind the neat exterior of this London house lies a duplex with the chic you would expect of Malcolm Livingstone, a restaurant proprietor whose restaurants are as renowned for their settings as their cuisine.

From a conventional series of two-up, two-down box rooms, Mr Livingstone persuaded his builder to remove large sections of Victorian brickwork and part of the slate roof at the back of the house. These were replaced with a glazed roof and a glass wall stretching from the ground floor to the eaves. The result is a shaft of light which tunnels down the building, lighting areas from the top landing staircase right down to the ground floor. The combined top and side light eliminates shadows so that everything is clearly seen. All the furniture in this area has been chosen to make defined shapes, while the glare from the glazed wall is controlled by a Luxaflex louvre blind. Soft apricot coloured walls, woodwork painted crisp white, and grey Wilton carpet unify the entire house and allow the exercise in style to commence.

The living space – it cannot be termed a room – occupies the whole of the ground floor, from the Victorian sash windows overlooking the street to the cathedral-like glass wall at the rear of the house. An observant eye in antique shops and salerooms can pick out the unusual piece, and Mr Livingstone has just such an eye. The pink and grey marble fireplace was found in the West Country and sparks off the colour theme for the furnishings.

An outstanding Biedermeier sofa sets a theatrical style – upholstered in a muted grey and red plaid, it almost fills the mirrored wall facing the fireplace. The mirror gives a double image of an oil painting of a clown by the American artist Michael Petringa, while a variety of antique chairs – each bought on its individual merit – have been upholstered in the same plaid or a faded gingham check from Claremont Fabrics. This fabric is also used to cover a glass-topped table between the sash windows, where a vast arrangement of alchemilla, sedum, eryngium and berries is punctuated by a few mauve- and pink-tinged asters and dahlia heads.

A pair of trestled-legged mahogany side tables on either side of the fireplace display a collection of marble

Geometric wallpaper above the chair rail and grey drag painting beneath combines with a Gothic framed mirror and library shelves (left) to make an outstanding bathroom design. Below: the piece of Gothic carving that triggered the design for the bookshelves, set at irregular levels to accommodate volumes of varying size.

and wooden columns. You need a collector's eye to search these out – one came from a demolished staircase, another was part of a carving from a ship and the third was a discarded lamp base. Grouped with prints of architectural details, they make a classical statement. The average-sized windows have been 'enlarged' using sixty metres of cream calico as generously trailing curtains. These were fashioned by David Hammond and designed to be permanently drawn back. In addition, for privacy, there are cream linen blinds

After the heavily curtained and mirrored end, the reverse view of this space is austere. A Gothic altar in pale wood serves as a sideboard for drinks, a single chair nearby echoes its Gothic shape, while a stark glass table, supported by a sturdy column base, gives a special sense to the dining area. Another superb find was the bust of Pope abandoned at the end of an auction. Beneath the garishly coloured effigy, Malcolm Livingstone saw the quality which would emerge when it was stripped of its many painted surfaces. It now stands as a cool presence by the glass table.

By removing the handrail and balustrade to the staircase, an open view has been gained of the collection of

Michael Petringa drawings of the human body that line the stairs. Malcolm Livingstone has chosen differing frames to give variety. Upstairs, in place of an enclosing wall, the bedroom has a balcony overlooking the stairwell, and as on the ground floor, the standard doors have been altered to give them extra width. A pair of American nineteenth-century primitive portraits of a man and a woman, in brown and white, gaze from either side of the tailored bed, which is flanked by pivoted, brown-shaded wall lamps.

After an air of detachment in the bedroom, the bathroom decor ensures that bathing is relaxing. The ubiq-

The tailored bedroom (below), set in the roof space, is lit by a roof light and a wall of glass at its far end.

The enclosing wall of the bedroom was removed to make a balcony (left) overlooking the stairwell and the glass 'wall'. The area is simply furnished with a tallboy and a cheval mirror; a plain curtain can be drawn to cut down the light. The tallboy holds an eye-level display of blue and white porcelain (below).

uitous fitted bathroom is a far cry from this drag-painted Gothic library retreat, whose cast-iron bath has been restored to its original glory. A piece of Gothic carving prompted the design for the frame of the book shelf, which is filled with favourite volumes and Staffordshire ornaments, while the basin is recessed in a console table. The half panelling and the woodwork have been drag painted in grey and a frieze detail added that copies the Gothic carving and edges geometrically patterned paper for the upper walls. The carved mahogany mirror also follows the pointed-arch theme.

All the decorative influences in this house pull in one direction, making a calm but stimulating environment for living. Mr Livingstone has also shown that with persistence it is possible to change totally the character of the building without extending the original space.

A Biedermeier sofa, upholstered in muted grey and red plaid, fills a mirrored recess (above), overlooked by Michael Petringa's painting of a clown. Left: a glass dining table stands on a column base, alongside a stone effigy of Pope that Livingstone found abandoned at the close of an auction.

A pink and grey marble fireplace in the living room (far left) acts as a pivot for an arrangement of architectural prints and wooden and marble columns.

A CLOCK HOUSE ON SOUTH DOWNS

◇

John Brookes runs his School of Garden Design from his residence and studio at the Clock House near Arundel, set at the foot of the South Downs. Converted from an early-nineteenth-century stable block, the house has been designed to merge with the surrounding gardens, and it is also a practical example of his theory that gardens should be designed to be part of the living area of the home.

A gravel matrix, used to grow plants in the rest of the garden, blends into the tones of the flint and brick Clock Hous (facing page). The arched entrance to the studio under the tower (right) forms part of an outside 'room'. Set in the angle of the building, this L-shaped terrace is designed to be part of the living area of the house.

John Brookes has had a significant influence on garden design over the last twenty years. His books on the subject have been published throughout the world and, through his School of Garden Design, students learn first-hand his basic gardening philosophies. Not surprisingly, his theories are practised at his home, which stands as part of the extraordinary gardens purchased originally from Lord Denman by Mrs J. H. Robinson and her husband. Mrs Robinson's passion has always been for the garden, which she created, section by section, over a period of thirty-five years.

At an age when most people are prepared to relax, Mrs Robinson started another brainchild. She wished the gardens at the Denmans to be a source of inspiration to

Above: a stone head and a sculpture fragment set beside plain stained windows in the studio, where the raised brick fireplace (right) is wide enough to burn huge logs.

others, and from his books and approach to garden design, John Brookes seemed the right 'heir' to continue them and help pass on her wisdom. He leased from her the old stable block which, with the assistance of architect Jonathan Manser, was turned into his residence and the School of Garden Design.

The simple stable structure of flint and brick dates from about 1820, but it also boasts the later addition of a clock tower. Clock House – so named by John Brookes – is separate from the Denman house, but planned so that

the gardens are shared yet ensure total privacy for each household. To appreciate the house, you need first to understand the philosophy of the gardens which surround it.

Though most people find a normal-sized garden difficult to manage, Mrs Robinson, nearing her eighties, was managing over three acres with the help of just one gardener. She pioneered a totally different approach to garden planning and this is the secret to managing vast areas. The key is to cultivate once, plant and then allow everything to ramble and seed itself into a gravel matrix. The only labour needed comes during the thinning out of what is not required, and the application of a late autumn dressing of well-rotted manure. Nature takes over and keeps the plant masses so tight that weeds rarely thrive. This could give the impression that the garden is wild, but that is not the case. Each corner and sweep has been meticulously 'painted' in its colour and shape by a gardening artist. If nature decides to sow seeds in the wrong part of the canvas, they are spotted and removed.

The gardens were extended into the pastureland, and a dry gravel stream was created to curve through it, planted with strong-foliaged plants that have been allowed to grow wild towards the extreme boundary. The old walled vegetable garden, whose conservatories flank the house, has been transformed into a magically beautiful flower and herb garden.

It is against this background of plants in sympathetic tonal and texture groupings that Clock House was converted into a home in harmony with its surroundings. The architect left the old buildings intact, even to the extent of leaving high stable windows as the source of daylight for the studio. Brown stain for all the woodwork leaves the natural tones of flint and brick to merge with the gravel matrix.

The entrance to the office end of the building is by a series of generous steps built of flagstones on a brick dais that provide varying heights for terracotta pots with plants. A small dormer window set in the slate roof has given this attic office views over the gardens of the Denman house.

Built in 1905, the clock tower has three brick arches that make a covered portico and an elegant main entrance to the house. Paving in this archway extends to make the south-facing corner of the house and conservatory wall into an extension of the living area; stable flooring bricks mixed with flagstones break the regularity here, while

Facing page: the view from the dining room looking out under the pergola to the terrace and grounds beyond. Stable bricks, interspersed with square paving, merge the house floor with that of the terrace. Hardwood slatted tables and chairs blend naturally into the garden, while this smooth area is broken by terracotta pots in a variety of shapes and sizes.

The pergola (above), bare in early spring to gain all the sunshine, is shaded in the summer by a vine.

A natural approach to decorating extends to the presentation of food. Lunch is laid on a woven cane table (above), alongside a pot of mixed polyanthus, bright cutlery and napkins, each echoing the colours of spring.

herbs contained in urns and pots delineate the edge of this terrace space.

A floor-to-ceiling window on the first floor and a matching one below light a bedroom and a dining room/kitchen at the most protected corner of the building, while a hardwood table and chairs left permanently outside furnish a garden dining area designed to capitalise on every hour of fine weather. Shade is provided by a pergola that allows vines to form a green roof at the end of the terrace.

The large area of the old stables has been turned into a lofty studio reaching up to the full height of the roof, while walls rendered in a natural stone colour and a pamment floor create a totally neutral background for creative thoughts. The working end of the studio has been designed to exclude any distractions from the garden views: work benches are evenly lit from a concealed source under a bookshelf, while daylight comes from the high stable windows. The line of the bench is continued as a book shelf to the fireplace recess at the other end of the room.

Heavy, square pedestals support giant urns for grass displays in two corners of the studio, and a simply constructed brick fireplace with a stone mantel is wide enough for a massive log fire, around which deep armchairs and sofas covered in linen are grouped to enjoy the warmth. In all, this important room is designed to produce an atmosphere of almost monastic calm to encourage original thought. Students who visit the Clock House for John Brookes' garden courses experience ideal conditions in which to gain from his expertise and the inspiration of the gardens surrounding the house.

Few house exteriors are creatively lit by night – the Clock House (above) is an exception. The lighting emphasizes the two entrances, managing to create a magical quality for the whole setting. Lights obscured behind plants throw beams up the building, highlighting the texture of the walls and throwing plants into delicate relief.

Groups of silver birch trees and shrubs in the lawn (right), due to be set in a sea of yellow later in the spring, when a variety of bulbs come into bloom.

Above: study work benches in the studio, designed away from the distracting views from the windows to aid students' concentration.

CONTINENTAL FLAVOUR IN A REGENCY VICARAGE

◇

Built in 1817 by the Hon. William Neville, this Regency house in Kent was lived in by a succession of vicars until 1946, when it was sold by the Church. The present owners have decorated their home in strong colours and a formal style to display their collection of Biedermeier and French Empire furniture. Seen from the outside, this residence still has the air of a country rectory, but the interior evokes an eclectic town house.

The imposing exterior of this Regency vicarage (facing page) faces onto a relaxed country garden. To the rear of the house, a clapboard addition is covered in a tangle of roses and creepers (right), half obscuring the windows on this elevation.

Deep green walls in the drawing room (right) are broken by a classical frieze that follows the chair rail and door frames. Formal groupings leave individual pieces of furniture to make separate statements – for example, a pair of Russian pale wood chairs and a single bergere are isolated from the tables and bookcase.

Below: a less formal view of the drawing room, with Paisley shawls covering the sofas and chairs.

T he Regency portico to the rectory opens onto a graceful, soft yellow hall whose original staircase and banisters curve up through the house. These curves are complemented by the smooth *bombé* shape of a Biedermeier chest in the hall following the sweep of the polished handrail. Wide, arched landings are accented with white against the mellow walls, which give space for the display of a collection of allegorical oil paintings in large, giltwood frames.

After the elegant introduction to the house, the visitor finds that, as a result of their love of Biedermeier and French Empire furniture, the owners have decorated their home in warm colours to enhance the pale tones of

walnut, birch, satinwood and fruit woods. Three intense shades of green are used for the living rooms downstairs, with Pompeian red for one bedroom and eggshell blue for another. By this emphasis on colour, the atmosphere of the house has been positively changed and, with the addition of this collection of European furniture, now recalls the formality of French houses in town settings.

The size of the drawing room ensures that it is not overwhelmed by the strength of the green chosen for the walls. A classical green and white frieze outlines the chair rail, door frames and ceiling mouldings, while heavy, plain curtains in an off-key green are simply treated for the generous bay sash window. A striking Biedermeier desk stands as a tall mass of polished wood, and when the desk is opened, fine craftsmanship is seen in the detailed drawers – the central one has been designed as an

Above: a neo-classical console table with solid column supports and a white marble top, matched in style with a wooden framed mirror decorated with parcel gilt. The tall Biedermeier desk (left), opened to show its fine craftsmanship, stands in a corner of the drawing room.

imposing entrance with steps, as though to a building. An impressive, neo-classical console table is a rare American piece, having solid column supports and a white marble top, and this is paired with a large mirror of parcel gilt design. English furniture creeps in with an octagonal table by Gillow (an ancestor of the present owners) set in the bay window to display a bronze of David and Goliath.

The formal placement draws attention to the furniture as individual pieces. A single bergere and a pair of Russian pale wood chairs are grouped with tables and a bookcase, while a pair of ebony and gilt candle holders stands on either side of an Empire clock surmounted by a sphinx. The sofas are softened with paisley shawls, and a lighter green is introduced by a display of Rathbone Della Robbia vases and plates.

Bright olive green is the background in the dining room for the heavier tones of mahogany. A Regency serving table of solid proportions is placed beneath a

Below: French Empire furniture set against Pompeian red walls in the bedroom, where classically hung, lichen green curtains form tails on three adjacent windows. An ornate ormolu and bronze chandelier lights the room with eight candles.

portentous oil painting of fishermen greeting their families. A three-fold screen with mirrored glass panels has been covered in the same fabric as the Morris-design curtains, and Regency-style furniture is interspersed with Art-Nouveau and Empire-style jugs, clocks and candle holders.

Away from the formality of these two rooms, the library is used as a private sitting room. Deep cream carpeting and khaki-coloured walls make an elegant setting for ebonised chairs upholstered in moire taffeta. Maple wood frames hold a set of engravings, while a charming oil of a family musical evening, framed in simple gilt, replaces the allegorical paintings in the main living rooms. The fireplace, set in a short, angled wall, is surrounded by brass scuttles and fenders, while a pair of Empire ormolu sphinx candles and a clock make dark silhouettes on a bookcase.

Above: a colour change to eggshell blue for a cool bedroom finished with natural silk blinds and curtains. The warm tone of the light wood furniture is enriched by a mustard coloured carpet.

Soft yellow walls and white
architrave details on the
stairwell and landings
(above) revive the dignity of
the Regency period. The small
library (right), carpeted in
deep cream with khaki
coloured walls, doubles as a
private sitting room.

From the graceful entrance
hall of the Rectory, the
original staircase curves up
through the house. These lines
are echoed in the curve of the
hall's Biedermeier chest (left).

The width of the Regency serving table in the dining room (right) is matched by an oil painting of fishermen.

Above: summer drinks on the terrace in the calm of an English country garden.

The swimming pool (right) is shielded from the Rectory by clipped hedges and a summer house, where the 'spade' symbol from a pack of cards is outlined in trellis work.

The French Empire bedroom is totally devoted to the style of this period. Napoleon's house at Malmaison, close to Paris, inspired the colour chosen for the walls – a deep Pompeian red, which has been coupled with white woodwork and a white ceiling to clear the glow. Lichen green curtains and white drapery with tails frame three windows at one end of the room. The bed, covered in white with a fine grey stripe, is French Empire, as is the marble-topped commode, while the additon of a pair of Regency inlaid chairs and wall lights marry these two styles.

A small, white fireplace holds an Empire-style four-pillar clock near a collection of engravings framed in maple, ebony and gilt. Two table lamps, one with a silver

Right: the trellis work below the clapboard bay used to make an enclosed garden porch.

column and the other in ormolu and bronze, but both having black shades, throw a clear light, but the main lighting of the room emanates from an ornate ormolu and bronze chandelier with eight lights.

From the rich glow of this bedroom, there is a cool change to eggshell blue for another room, which has natural silk Roman blinds and curtains, and blue upholstery on an armchair and on an occasional chair set at the dressing table. A mustard-coloured carpet brings out the warm tones of the wood.

Whilst giving the interior a distinctively foreign formality, the owners have left the grounds as a relaxed English country garden. The symmetry of the Regency facade of the house has been broken by later additions, although not all of these are without merit. For example, a white, clapboarded square bay at the rear gives additional views of the garden for one bedroom, having windows set on three sides. Beneath them is a garden porchway covered in creepers and vines, and a magnificent magnolia reaching to roof height. Indeed, with sweeping green lawns, shrubberies and large trees, this residence has all the dignity of a quiet country rectory set in 'The Garden of England'.

AWARD-WINNING RESTORATION

◆

Fifteenth-century Bentley Hall was nearing collapse when it was found by the Harwoods. Their meticulous study of architectural records dating back to 1475, and of paintings of Spanish and Dutch interiors, guided the restoration of this timber-framed house. The building won an award as one of the three finest conversions in Suffolk in the 1975 Architectural Heritage Year Awards, and it is now considered to be one of East Anglia's most exceptional small manor houses.

When Wendy and Richard Harwood bought Bentley Hall in 1973 the building was in danger of losing its roof and flattening part of the house as it fell. This was the wing the agents had recommended should be demolished. At this time the Harwoods were living in a large Georgian mansion they had decided to leave because the local authority planned to flood the valley for a reservoir. The agent's particulars mentioned a small Regency house with a 'derelict bit' at the back so, as it was close to their home, they decided to inspect it and discovered that the agent did not appreciate the architectural value of the building. The 'derelict' wing was a once-splendid, fifteenth-century hall.

The task of rescuing the building could have overwhelmed the faint hearted. The Harwoods had a family of five children and Richard Harwood ran a dairy farm. Although they had restored several homes before, nothing matched the scale or type of structure of Bentley. Detailed research was needed to find architectural records dating from the fifteenth century, and the Harwoods also decided that, with such a complex structure, they needed direct contact with the craftsmen, so Richard controlled the building labour himself, with

Above: a snow-covered figure in the walled garden. The massive timbers used for a pair of archways (facing page) can be seen from the main hall.

architectural supervision. A partner in the chosen firm of architects understood timber-framed buildings and, with his guidance, original windows and archways hidden under layers of later construction were found with uncanny accuracy.

The major priority was to save the main roof. The structure was stripped to the bare timbers at the danger points and ships' hawser ropes were fixed to stop the walls falling out further from the vertical. These were then slowly tightened until the roof could be secured back onto the wall plates. It was clear that the structure had been within inches of disaster.

Infinite patience and enthusiasm for the slow work carried the project forward. Hidden doorways and windows, suggested by faint lines, were cause for great

A gilt lantern of Gothic design (above) hangs in the stairwell.

Right: the fifteenth-century wing of Bentley Hall.

celebrations when unearthed, and when the roof was secured, the Harwoods held a house-warming party for friends in the open structure. This methodical way of slowly uncovering the architecture of the house took just over a year, and the work was like an archaeological dig. The original brick floor was found in the kitchen and meticulously relaid. A Tudor arch was concealed beneath a Victorian fireplace, and when everything was pulled away a magnificent walk-in brick fireplace was uncovered. After a lot of research, the Hall floor was copied from the decorative design of a sixteenth-century chateau using old material from a demolished maltings.

Furnishings in the main hall (top) leave the strength and scale of the architecture unimpaired. Above: Belgian tapestry. Right: the upper hall, which shares the chimney with the floor below.

The family moved in after six months, their furniture and possessions stacked around rubble. The task of decorating the home started in the Georgian wing, which had three bedrooms, a library and a sitting room. As their previous homes had all been of the same period, the style came as second nature to Wendy Harwood, their furniture and possessions easily settling into the new environment to give it a mellow, lived-in look. Gentle yellow, warm browns and soft blues act as cohesive agents in shaping the rooms.

Ideas for the immense hall and timbered rooms above did not come so easily, as normal-sized furniture and pictures clearly would be lost in the space. Wendy Harwood set about the creative task methodically. She studied paintings of sixteenth-century Dutch and Spanish interiors at the National Gallery, collecting postcards of Holbein and De Hooch paintings. These she researched carefully at home until she found details she liked and worked out if it was possible to create these in the twentieth century.

The key was muted colours, rich tapestries and well-thought-out groups of furniture. Grey linen hangings with a hint of green on dull metal rods quietly dress the windows, their presence making no visual demands to detract from the fenestration. A large, classically styled sofa, upholstered in blue grey, is set against the long window and guarded by two classical busts on the intricately laid brick floor, while another stands on a marble column.

Perspective is given to the length of the hall by the large, sixteenth-century Belgian tapestry that hangs between the library and sitting room doors. Oriental rugs and a large, blue carpet are left in an open space, while sofas form a comfortable group round the stone fireplace. No attempt has been made to visually reduce the size of the room. The Harwoods have left the eloquence of the massive-beamed ceiling and surrounding architecture to speak for itself.

The family dining table in the kitchen could easily be fitted into the giant fireplace. In fact, an armchair is left permanently inside the chimney breast so that one may enjoy the warmth of the burning logs. The narrow Tudor bricks, laid in a chevron pattern on the floor, give a lovely, soft patina. It is very much a family room, having a large pine dresser filled with a collection of china and pottery made by one of the Harwoods' daughters.

Below: a view from the sitting room into the library.

Left: a clever grouping of dark and light tones uses a portrait and papier maché tray behind a classical stone bust.

The warm-toned drawing room (below) is a later addition to Bentley Hall.

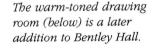

The staircase had to be reconstructed and the timber was found from a variety of sources. Newel posts were discovered in the garden, banisters were provided by a local pub in the course of alteration and the treads were constructed from the solid wooden piles used to moor ships in the docks. It makes an authentic and highly ingenious staircase. Family portraits hang on the plain walls, and the stairs are lit with an elegant, glass storm lantern.

The upper hall is almost long enough to hold a race. The Oriental carpets were bought at auctions at bargain prices, and have the appropriately worn-in look for the house. A longcase clock with rich inlay, a twin chairback settee and several other chairs, plus a large tallboy and an oak chest are almost lost in the space. The faint aroma of burning wood greets you as you come up the stairs, as the

Above: a china and pottery collection in the kitchen and (below) rope ties on plush curtains.

Above right: a Napoleonic bedroom where a French Empire bed is recessed in the blue-striped Regency room.

central fireplace shares the chimney with the main fire in the hall below.

Three differing bedrooms lead off the hallway. Warm peach covers the panelling in one, with lines painted in grey to delineate the panels. A William IV bed painted grey with a green line pattern is covered with a fabric stencilled with a pineapple design, which has also been copied for the curtains and carefully placed cushions.

A door further down the hallway leads to a Napoleonic bedroom. Here the walls are covered in blue Regency stripe, while the French Empire bed has been set in a very inviting alcove painted in soft terracotta. The alcove is curtained with a beige and white fabric and finished with a navy fringe.

The third room is in clear blue and white. The unusual placing of the four-poster bed in the middle of the window makes it the main feature. Though its drapes are

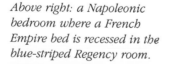

plain blue, edged in flowered braid, the inner hangings are pure white and teamed with a lace coverlet. The upper half of the white, panelled walls are papered in a blue, patterned stripe.

With so much space, the decoration could provide the Harwoods with an absorbing pastime searching out more and more objects. It is fortunate the owners started with a large collection of family portraits and mementos, for Wendy Harwood has been able carefully to group these possessions in relationship tableaux, so preserving the threads of the family history. Their energy then turned to restoring a beautifully timbered barn, set a short distance behind the Hall, and to landscaping the gardens. Wide terraces from the barn lead down to a pond dug with a small island in the centre. Reached by a chinoiserie bridge, it will allow future owners to look up to Bentley Hall and marvel at the diligence and care which went into the restoration.

Above: a four-poster bed, backlit by a massive window in the blue and white room. Painted stencil techniques are a feature in this bedroom (right), where line painting on the William IV bed is repeated on the panelled walls and the same pineapple stencil design is found on the bedcover, cushions and curtains.

A SEVENTEENTH-CENTURY HALL IN YORKSHIRE

The Old Town Hall, standing a thousand feet above the Yorkshire town of Hebden Bridge, is an interesting example of the type of house built in the early part of the seventeenth century in the bleak areas of the Yorkshire moors. Constructed of stone, these solid buildings were made to stand up to the bleak winter weather, and this hall has withstood the passing centuries with most of its architectural details intact.

Flowers have been an essential part of Derek Bridges' life for the past twenty years. He has written two books on the art of flower arranging and spends most of his time on lecture tours both in England and abroad. When he is at home, he and his wife enjoy cultivating from seed the plants of specific interest to flower arrangers. As texture and form rate highly on their list of priorities, it is not surprising that the Bridges' home seems protected by greenery.

Set on a hillside above Hebden Bridge, the Old Town Hall was built around 1600 on the site of an earlier wooden house, which was recorded as far back as 1390. Records show that a secret passage, which led to a copse of trees several fields away, existed behind the stone fireplace in the dining room, although it has now collapsed with earth falls over the years.

Houses in this area of Yorkshire were built to withstand the damp climate of the moors, and they were constructed to last. Low roofs of massive gritstone flags, stone-mullioned windows with label moulds over them to carry the water away, and gritstone masonry built in

The owner's love of foliage softens the solid stone hall (facing page) and twines round a statue (above) in the garden.

A path of well-worn York paving stones (right) leads from the house through the garden, where urns set on pedestals bring bright colours to a background of rich greens.

In an intimate corner of the garden stands a white metal seat (below), almost hidden by variegated ivy and shrubs.

strong, horizontal courses all contribute to the dour character of seventeenth-century houses in this region. The Old Town Hall has these early architectural qualities, weathered black over the centuries, but now lightened and softened by the present owner's love of plants.

Variegated ivy covers the imposing porch entrance, and carefully planted cupressus trees and laurels form an avenue either side of the well-worn York paving stones leading from the front door to the Tudor stone arch in the garden wall. Urns planted with variegated ivy and

brilliant red geraniums make a strong splash of colour against the mixture of green texture and darkened stone. *Alchemilla mollis* adds a soft yellow feather edging to the stone path.

Stone pathways form curved corners for groups of hostas and a variety of green groundcover, punctuated by tall lilies. As Derek Bridges is interested in texture and shape in foliage, he takes care that the garden does not decline in the winter, and small, intimate, evergreen corners make interesting patterns, sometimes with the introduction of statues and pebbles.

Although the house has plenty of long windows, the nature of stone mullion frames means that interiors are low on light, and artificial lighting is a contributory factor in the decoration. With the exception of the hall, rich-toned colours have been chosen. The black and white tile floor in the entrance hall dictates the rest of the colour scheme there – white and black. A marble-topped console table with a mirrored back has an elegant giltwood mirror standing upon it. Black, figure-based lamps either side of a silver and bronze arrangement make glittering reflections in the glass dome, while a large marble statue aids this theatrical entrance. Mirror images of the stairs, collages by Derek Bridges and black-shaded lamps increase the hall's depth.

A cloisonné vase doubles as a lamp base (right), and is grouped with an alabaster ewer and vase in the sitting room. The delicate colours of a peperomia houseplant echo the shades in the lamp.

Left: a display of navy and white china fills an arched recess (left), where a large meat plate and a collection of teapots have been placed to echo the curve.

Below: the black and white entrance hall presents highly contrasting tones and shapes.

Above: a glass-fronted cupboard stands with the doors wide to display a collection of green Wedgwood pottery and Art Deco vases and boxes.

The mood changes abruptly in the sitting room, with strong green walls and Victorian velvet-upholstered chairs. Among such rich tones, the use of white needs handling with care. Low lighting and a white ceiling produce strong light in the room. A glass-fronted display cupboard lined in green moire taffeta holds an interesting collection of green Wedgwood pottery, while a large Cloisonne vase in rich blue, decorated with birds and blossoms, makes an imposing table lamp by the window.

The rich green follows through to the dining room, though only for the carpet. Here the use of creams acts as a quiet foil to the oak beams, the stone fireplace and the mullioned windows. The ornately carved dining table can accommodate a large gathering, seated at the pew bench and high-backed chairs with upholstered seats. A panel-back chair and footstool stand in the corner near a pair of large ceramic columns that act as bases for a splendid pair of lamps made from statues of horsemen. Simple cream curtains hang by the stone window frames.

The beamed guest bedroom upstairs has a cosy style in which cream walls complement pale, delicate, flower-sprigged quilts and curtains, and hung above the headboards of the twin beds are a pair of dried flower collages in round mahogany frames. In addition, this room has one of the original stone windows with leaded lights. Another bedroom has also been designed to give a fresh Victorian country feel, having a pine double bedstead and winged chair. Rosebud-sprigged paper has been used to cover the walls and ceiling between the black beams, there are matching curtains and quilt covers, and three ribbon plates, slotted with pink ribbon, hang on the walls.

The kitchen (right) is designed to retain the dark wood of the old building. Storage shelves form a series of arches, while the very top shelf displays large pieces of china.

The original stone fireplace in the dining room (above) once hid the entrance to a secret passage. The owners have retained the period atmosphere of the room by using heavy, carved furniture and hanging simple curtains at the mullioned windows.

Above: rich Victorian colours in the sitting room.

Left: a view of the living room, where rich tones are offset by blocks of white.

Right: a Victorian, country-style bedroom, where one pattern of rosebud sprigs unifies the space around the pine bed.

Below: the master bedroom, the bed splendidly set in a curtained recess. The tones of soft lemon, coral pink and green merge the walls and curtains into one background for the bed.

The master bedroom has the bed set in a 'stage'. A solid floral print of coral mixed with pink and green covers the walls, while the ceiling is soft cream. Curtains of matching print, generously full with frilled edges, are draped either side of the bed recess and the stone mullioned windows. A continuous, frilled valance runs across the beam above the bed and the window, while the alcove is lit by warm-toned lamps on the long shelf, which is part of the carved wooden headboard. A large bowl of dried pink and grey flowers stands on a bamboo whatnot to complete the scheme.

The owners' shared interest in flowers shows in their equal treatment of the house and garden, and indeed, the present garden is very much a part of the beauty of the Old Town Hall today. A perfectionist might condemn the mixture of periods and styles, but the owners enjoy the qualities of their period house which they have furnished to their personal taste and comfort. If they have the space, finance and inclination, they include what they like without bowing to the dictates of one particular style.

Above: the guest bedroom, where the oak beams and one of the original stone windows are set against plain colours.

Open shelves at varying heights (above) provide ample storage and allow easy access.

CASTLE DROGO, BUILT BY SIR EDWIN LUTYENS

✧

Castle Drogo is a monument to the eccentricity of an Edwardian Englishman and the work of one of Britain's most famous architects. The castle is the dream of a man who retired in his thirties, having made his own fortune, and it was designed by Sir Edwin Lutyens. Built over a period of twenty years, from 1910 to 1930, it stands today as a fitting tribute to them both.

Julius Drewe was sent by his family to learn the art of business trading at the age of seventeen. As the tea trade was at its height, most of his training took place abroad. On returning to England he realised it was more profitable to buy products direct from the producer, and on this basis he started his own business in Liverpool when he was just twenty-two. After five years of successful trading, he took on a partner, moved the company's centre to London and, under the name of Home and Colonial Stores, founded a chain of buying houses. The following six years of enormous trading success were sufficiently lucrative for Drewe to retire from work at the age of thirty-three, one of the wealthiest self-made men in Liverpool.

In 1890 he purchased his first castle, and shortly afterwards another large house. Having discovered an interest in architecture, and driven on by the proverb 'An Englishman's home is his castle', he decided he wanted to build a fortress of his own.

He found the ideal piece of land – a large plateau with the ground falling away sharply on three sides, and easy

Left: the massive exterior of Castle Drogo, built on a plateau, and (above) the imposing tower entrance, with the family emblem carved in a granite slab.

Left: a round, leather-topped drum table set with period desktop equipment. Facing page top: the fortress outline of Lutyens' building set against a dark Dartmoor sky.

Facing page bottom: the castle's open granite fireplace and timbered ceiling that are both on a vast scale. The staircase (below) has a nine-metre-high window. Doors on the right lead to the dining room, and to an internal staircase connecting the owners' private rooms.

access for building on the fourth – so with just one contract he purchased 150 hectares of hills and valleys on the edge of Dartmoor, the forbidding moor in south Devon. Another 350 hectares were added to the estate at a later date.

In the summer of 1910, when Drewe met Sir Edwin Lutyens, the latter had just been commissioned by the Government to build a palace for the British Viceroy in India. It was against this scale of project that Castle Drogo was undertaken. Lutyens' previous largest private commission had been to build a house for Hemingway with a budget of £17,500. Julius Drewe gave the order that £60,000 be made available for the building of his castle – in those days an incredible amount to be spent on a private residence. He considered £50,000 should be allocated to the building and £10,000 to the grounds, and on 4th April, 1911, his birthday, the foundation stone of Castle Drogo was laid.

Shortly afterwards, requests for alterations to plans started to be made, which involved technical problems. Drewe insisted that his castle should be made of solid granite, against the advice of the architect, who knew this would escalate the costs. The owner's wishes prevailed, but it meant that the building had to be scaled down from the original plans. However, building work continued despite changing plans, and the two men became friends. The First World War came and went, and it was agreed that the plans should be reduced yet again, so work re-started with a smaller workforce. Castle Drogo was finally completed eleven years later in 1930. The owner had one year to enjoy the literal truth of the proverb before he died.

Members of the family still live at Drogo, but it is now owned by the National Trust, an organisation involved with the preservation of buildings of historic interest. It is therefore possible for visitors to see this incredible *folie de grandeur* of a young, self-made businessman, executed by one of Britain's finest architects, and to enjoy the furniture which belongs to the period.

As the foundations were laid for a house double the size of the completed castle, Lutyens still retained his original concept in scale for the huge entrance. The tower, with two strong pillars at either corner, has the family emblem of a lion passant carved in a granite slab larger than the castle entrance. The granite for the construction of the building was mined from a nearby quarry and carried to

Portraits of Julius Drewe (above) and his wife (top) hang at opposite ends of the barrel-vaulted hall. Dinner parties at Castle Drogo required a retinue of servants to carry dishes to the dining room (right) from the kitchen thirty-five metres away.

the site by the special railway built to carry all the building materials to the plateau. As a finishing touch to the rather grim exterior, a portcullis – the grid designed to repel marauding enemies – was installed so that it could be lowered over the entrance by Julius Drewe.

The barrel-vaulted hall provides an impressive connection between the entrance and the well of the stairs leading down to the dining room on the lower floor. Having a nine-metre-high window, its scale is nearer to that of a church than a home. The differing sizes and shapes of the granite blocks used to make the structured ceiling are a testament to Lutyens' design skill, making this part of the castle of prime architectural interest.

The granite, left bare in the entrance and on the stairs, is covered with polished wooden floors and dark wall panelling in the dining room, where solid upright beams support wooden ceiling moulding. A long table set with white damask and electric silver candles (the cables are concealed beneath the table) could accommodate twelve guests. The food for this entertainment would have had to be carried the thirty-five metres separating the dining room from the kitchen.

The kitchen on the lower floor receives all its daylight from a dome in the ceiling and the high-set windows in the arched, vaulted roof. Wooden draining racks for china are recessed into the granite walls above a long series of sinks set in slate. The furniture for the kitchen is part of the architectural design; here a vast dresser is set into the granite walls too, its shelves supported by the granite, while a sloping back shelf holds a row of jugs of decreasing sizes.

Cooking was done on two enormous ranges and meals prepared on a table designed by Lutyens. It was carried to the pantry (half-way between the kitchen and dining room), arranged for serving there, and then carried to the guests in the dining room. It was fortunate that Castle Drogo has central heating, as the logistics of serving hot food must have been a nightmare! Half a dozen employees worked in the kitchen to cope with the task.

Despite the central heating, of course, the castle had to have a great baronial fireplace, and this was destined to be one of the biggest in the country. Built entirely of granite, it is set off-centre in the room with a panelled wood ceiling. Due to the scale of Drogo, which was soon of equal standing with royal residences, nineteen servants were needed to run the house efficiently.

The structured paths and lawns follow the lines of the exterior (above) and are bare of the softening influence of foliage.

One of the castle's many bathrooms contains an interesting period piece of plumbing. The white bath has an elegant porcelain curved screen, finished with copper knobs, standing at the end of the bath to direct shower water. The details of the mullioned windows set high in the room and the views from them were designed to be observed via a series of raised dais steps, covered in wood, which also hold a collection of well-polished water jugs.

At least seven people are needed to care for the grounds, planned to protect the garden from the strong west and southwest winds. The gardens were laid out in a symmetry in keeping with that of the building. Shingle paths, edged with granite, and immaculate, straight-edged lawns are protected by metre-thick hedges of yew. An enclosed and protected garden of roses and shrubs is approached via a series of terraces from the castle. In each corner is a seat under a large arched trellis surrounded by hedges and here a far vista of Dartmoor is seen through a narrow tunnel of high yew hedges.

Julius Drewe did not live to see the fruition of his garden plans, but his driving force, which carried the project on over so many years, gave rise to a unique architectural monument for others to appreciate today. His presence is still very much felt at Castle Drogo, as over-life-size portraits of both him and his wife hang at either end of his awe-inspiring hall.

Above: the scale of the great barrel-vaulted roof balances the nine-metre-high window.

Below: the kitchen, where light floods in from a dome in the ceiling and food was prepared on two large ranges.

Below: a pestle and mortar and (bottom) an ascending series of hooks for hanging jugs of increasing size.

Meticulously fashioned
granite arches in the hall
(left) make an impressive
setting for an elaborately
carved gong beside the dining
room entrance. The scale of
Sir Edwin Lutyens' windows
(above) is even more
impressive at dusk.

Above: door furniture
especially designed for Castle
Drogo.

LEIGHTON HALL IN LANCASHIRE

◆

Lancashire is not a county renowned for its light-hearted architecture – plain, no-nonsense buildings are nearer to the mark. As a consequence, one's first sight of Leighton Hall comes as a shock, as it looks just like a cut-out castle for a stage setting. Indeed, disorientation can beset visitors to this hall, which is hardly surprising as successive generations have left their mark with contrasting additions to this Adam-style building. Apart from the historical interest of the building, though, the house is worthy of note as it contains a unique collection of furniture specially designed for the house by the Gillow family, and still in use by their descendants today.

Facing page: the Victorian wing of Leighton Hall, viewed from across the lake. The long facade of the hall (above) is set as if on a dais amid rolling pastureland.

Since 1246, when records show a fortified manor on the site, there has always been a hall at Leighton. The present building was built in 1763 in the classic, Adam style. Half a decade on, another owner added a neo-Gothic facade (producing a contradiction of periods on entering the hall), while another proud owner added his mark by building a Victorian wing and conservatory in 1870. In this manner, it has grown into a rambling fantasy home much loved by the Gillow family, who have lived here for generations. The hall is now open to the public to help towards the cost of maintaining such a sprawling inheritance, but it is clear one is visiting a cherished family home, not a museum.

Apart from the history of the building, the furniture here is of special interest as the hall was owned by the Gillows of Lancaster, the family behind the famous furniture business that later became Waring and Gillow of London. The house still contains many of the best craftsman-made pieces that were brought to Leighton when Richard Gillow, grandson of the furniture-founder Robert Gillow, purchased the hall in 1822.

Though successive generations marked their stay with dramatic changes in architecture, the present owners, Richard and Suzie Gillow Reynolds, simply wish to cherish these gathered family possessions and the

Far left: light from the glass-panelled front door and windows shines on an unusual daisy shaped table in the hall. Above: gothic tracery makes soft patterns of yellow light in the entrance hall, where a coat stand is engulfed with family outdoor wear.

Deep pink hydrangea blooms (above) flourish in a tub washed the same blue as a garden door.

The library (left) has acquired the personal collections of successive generations, with portraits and pictures filling nearly all the available space on the green walls. A curved bookcase area has been filled with leather volumes, while the arch shelves remain a safe home for special porcelain.

The panelled dining room (right) is a mixture of rich browns – colours that have been chosen so as not to detract from the wooden dining furniture. This furniture spans over a century of craftsmanship: the carved chairs were made in 1671, the leather-seated dining chairs were designed by Robert Gillow in 1735 and the long, polished Gillow table is late eighteenth century.

Above: a lectern-shaped coin cabinet set on tripod legs.

Left: the library, a room for all members of the family to use, including the dogs.

Above: the music room, where shades of pink are drawn together by silk flowers and dried gypsophila on the grand piano.

memories they evoke. The well-worn patinas are not going to be sharpened with designs of the present era; style is going to be allowed to stand still during their guardianship of the family home.

The visitor's introduction to Leighton Hall starts at the amazing, double door entrance set with windows of Gothic tracery and stained glass. Once in the vestibule, a relaxed collection of coats and gumboots is found, and this is how the owners intend visitors should view the Hall, as a living family home. The window tracery here casts lovely patterns on the soft yellow walls, while the inner hall door has a high arch with tracery and rich Victorian plush curtains used to exclude draughts. The diagonally laid grey stone slabs have well-worn blue rugs upon which a unique piece of furniture stands. Thought to have been designed as a gaming table, it has curved, fold-down wings that form a daisy outline. All around the soft yellow walls are displayed antler and mask trophies of a previous inhabitant's hunting prowess, collections of family portraits and landscape paintings.

Slender Gothic pillars form arches with more tracery to support the upper landing of the magnificent, canti-levered staircase. This makes a graceful sweep upwards into a vaulted space at the far end of the hall, its plain metal balustrades held by a wooden handrail. Sunlight shining through the stained-glass window casts coloured gems of light onto the bare, stone treads, while the period is maintained with a Gothic red leather armchair.

The oak-panelled dining room might almost be a museum setting of furniture, but for the fact that it is used frequently for candlelit dinner parties. Having also been used as a billiard room at one point, the pattern mouldings on the ceiling are interrupted by a round roof light which lightens the dark walls. The long, polished Gillow table dates from the late-eighteenth century, the leather-seated dining chairs were made in 1735 by Robert Gillow (founder member of the furniture firm), while the massive carver chairs were made in 1671. Thus the furniture collection spans over one-hundred-and-twenty-five years of craftsman-made furniture.

The library at Leighton Hall is a comfortable gathering place for family and friends. Leather-bound volumes are arranged on bookshelves in arched recesses, the curved top shelf used for displaying china. Almost every available space on the soft green walls is covered with family portraits and gilt-framed pictures. Sofas and armchairs,

Above: a black-tiled bathroom with Art Deco influences.

Above: the drawing room's coal fire.

Gillow Reynolds. Duttons of Chester made a bird's-eye maple wood suite for Lady Reynolds, grandmother of the present owner, in 1860. The bed is hung in heavy ecru lace and draped with dove grey fabric held by lace roses, while a matching chest of drawers, dressing table and wardrobe complete the bridal suite. This period piece is used frequently as a guest room.

Away from furniture, the bathroom is Art Deco, having a pedestal basin and curve-edged bath. The walls are fitted with black, oblong mirror tiles to three quarter height in the room, and above that they have been painted green. The music room has parquet floors, left free of carpeting, and an interesting period touch here is the bowl of silk flowers placed on the grand piano. The Victorian conservatory, used as a greenhouse for house-plants, has a colonnaded verandah covered in wisteria to join it to the earlier building.

Every skyline view of Leighton Hall is broken by castellated roofs and turrets, and day-to-day maintenance of a such a large-scale home must be an overwhelming task. The threat of major roof repair is ever present, but fortunately the present generation have the energy to tackle the unending task, keeping their home open to the public in order to raise the funds. They are determined to preserve the family tradition at Leighton Hall, so resisting the temptation to move with the times, and certainly so far they have been successful in their aim.

with loose covers in deep rose, are filled with practical cushions chosen for comfort and, as successive generations have added their personal collections, the room is now filled with Gillow memories.

The drawing room possesses a sharpened version of the faded charm of Leighton Hall. Used as the location for a television series, the room was given a heightened Victorian character by the use of heavily patterned blue chintz and a coral carpet. The armchairs are set formally round the room as conversation pieces, alongside a work table and side tables. The windows, which frame a view of the Lakeland hills in the distance, are swathed in soft drapes of fine lace, while a gaming table from the early eighteenth century and a Kentia palm in a brass urn act as elegant focal boundaries.

Few families can boast that their grandmother's bridal suite remains in their home, but that is the case for the

Enhanced by their delicate lace curtains, the drawing room windows (above left) provide uninterrupted views of the Lakeland hills. The games table is early-eighteenth-century Gillow. At the far end of the hall lies an elegant, cantilevered staircase (right), graced by a Gothic stained-glass window set centrally up the first sweep of stairs.

The decoration at Leighton Hall (this page) has grown with the years. Nothing intrudes to mar the space and calm of a family home, respected by successive generations.

THE REVIVAL OF CHARLESTON

✦

Charleston Farm in Sussex was home to the writers and artists of the Bloomsbury Group from 1916 to the late Sixties. Much has been written about Virginia Woolf, her sister Vanessa Bell and the inter-related members of the group, the principal characters of which formed a strong literary and artistic influence on the early part of this century. From the written records it is possible to follow the pattern of their lives, but little cohesive visual material remains. At Charleston, the Charleston Trust is, piece by piece, putting together the mosaic of their creative lives.

I n 1916 Virginia and her husband Leonard Woolf were living at Asham in Sussex. The members of the Bloomsbury Group were pacifists and many obtained exemption from war service on condition they undertook full-time agricultural work. Vanessa Bell, her artist friend Duncan Grant and David Garnett were striving to run a farm in Suffolk, and after Virginia discovered Charleston down a chalk lane close to Firle in Sussex, her sister and this 'retinue' decided to move there in October 1916. Their home, which started as a wartime retreat, turned into a magnet for all the talented members of the Bloomsbury Group It continued to draw artists during the Twenties and Thirties, and their free expression of art – not just on canvas, but also on furniture, pottery and walls – embodies their colourful lives. The brightness of this era finally faded with the death of Vanessa in 1961 and that of Duncan Grant in 1978, when the lease was relinquished to Charleston's owners.

A trust was formed to buy, restore and preserve the house and garden, and today art lovers are able to

The studio (left) at Charleston (above) was built in 1925 and its walls decorated by Duncan Grant.

Above and right: the matt black walls of the dining room act as a foil to the rich tones of the pictures, painted furniture and pottery. A painted table made at Omega called Lilypond (left) has been placed with a William Morris rush settee in one of the main rooms overlooking the garden.

experience the extraordinary talents of these British artists through their life style at Charleston.

This asymmetric farmhouse, the South Downs rising steeply behind it, was built in the eighteenth century. Its protected position almost makes the garden of equal importance to the house, and the idyllic summers that were spent there are reflected in the artists' work. Vanessa Bell had her room on the ground floor, and so was free to wander at any time in the garden she so loved.

First impressions on walking into Charleston are of mellow walls and tiled floors redolent of Provence, with a spice of sophistication. In the hallway a brooding Buddha on a chinoiserie table and a battered rush chair stand in front of an Italian gilt mirror.

Clive Bell, Vanessa's husband, was a leading art critic. His friend Roger Fry had a consuming passion to bring to the English middle classes an awareness of the worth of the Postimpressionists, but, as they seemed unable to accept the visual 'assault' in art form, he hoped a similar movement in decoration might succeed. He had opened the Omega Workshops in 1913 to make Postimpressionist

Above: Duncan Grant's bedroom – the fireplace tiles were designed by Vanessa Bell.

Below: an almost lifesize painting of food being prepared in the kitchen.

furniture, curtains, cushions and lampshades, and his designs from Omega can be seen at Charleston.

The dining room is painted matt black to act as a foil for the rich tones of the paintings and furniture, and as such, the room is a complete expression of the Bloomsbury Group, who believed that art was to be enjoyed and used. They met for meals at the large circular table decorated by Vanessa in naïve patterns. Roger Fry made the set of cane chairs with red-painted frames at Omega, and he also designed the fireplace alcove to form niches for a ceramic and pottery collection, while Vanessa Bell's presence is felt in this room by her powerful self-portrait that hangs above the Kirkman harpsichord.

Clive Bell's study on the ground floor is washed in sunflower yellow, and has a moss green chimney breast and ceiling. This is a quieter room than most, but it still exudes creative energy in its decorated fireplace and window panels. Even the coal box can boast a lively Matisse figure, while a Dutch inlaid table and a fine

Empire chair give a sophisticated contrast to the naïve panels.

One of the main rooms near the entrance overlooks the round pool in the garden, and the reflected light from this increases the atmosphere of Charleston. A vividly painted table – called Lilypond – was made at Omega and is placed alongside a William Morris rush settee by the window. Maynard Keynes used this room, while in another quiet room in the house he wrote *Economic Consequences of the Peace*, and his faded yellow work files are kept in a hand-painted bookcase. Indeed, the literary influence is as strong as the artistic. The library on the first floor has bookcases filled with classics and French yellowbacks and Duncan Grant decorated the book-shelves and the window panels with a giant wolfhound and pheasant.

The studio was added to the house by Roger Fry in 1925, and is perhaps its most exciting room. Around seven metres long, with ceiling-height windows and a north light, it was an artist's inspiration. Duncan Grant started decorating the walls as soon as it was built, and two languid figures alongside a huge fishbowl gaze from the fireplace into this room that has housed so much talent. Grant's work is emblazoned with vibrant colours that merge with the sharp primary colours of the painted furniture – the studio has decorated cupboards and country chairs chequer-boarded with matt colour.

It is perhaps in the bedrooms that the group's attitude to life is most apparent. They had an irreverent regard for

A Post Impressionist influence is clear in one of the guest bedrooms (left and above). Soft, warm colours merge in the wall and window patterns and on the freely decorated furniture.

antiques, believing that they were to be casually used and enjoyed and therefore freely applied with colour. A Louis XVI bedstead in Clive Bell's room was painted by Vanessa, while another bedhead was decorated by Grant with images of Morpheus, the god of sleep. The influence of the Postimpressionists on the Bloomsbury set has left its mark on one of the guest rooms too. Soft, warm colours merge on walls and window panels, while most of the furniture has been liberally covered with colour and designs.

This freedom of expression spreads to the spartan bathroom, as there are voluptuous paintings on the iron bath tub. Even the doors did not escape their brush strokes. A simple, planked door is embellished with a Grecian figure in muted pinks and mauves, while a table top has been decorated with a boy astride a dolphin.

Charleston holds visual images of the people themselves, too. Self-portraits, a portrait of Virginia and Vanessa's brother Adrian Stephens and the austere head of Virginia by Stephen Tomlin grace the walls. Shut off from the outside world, apart from the daily visits of the Lewes mail van, they lived an almost charmed life. Clive Bell would be busy with his art reviews, Vanessa spent most of her time in the garden, painting or tending the plants, Duncan Grant worked in the studio and Quentin Bell was busy with his kiln. The charisma of the place drew other members of the Bloomsbury group, and Virginia Woolf regularly visited her sister when she was well enough to make the trip from Asham. The house was not simply somewhere to live, it was their life.

Possibly much of the allure lay in the garden. It is being re-constructed now, and from Vanessa's paintings it

was evidently planted with freedom in its colour and shape – presumably Vanessa disliked controlled gardens. Statues were also placed there – with humour. A brick pillar is curved at the top into a figure of a woman, a marble statue grows out of the middle of a box hedge, and a reclining figure by the pool is half-hidden by cow parsley.

This living decoration and visual garden image of an epoch in British art is an intriguing addition to the wealth of literary records. The personal collections of Virginia Woolf, Vanessa Bell, Duncan Grant, Roger Fry, Clive and Quentin Bell have all been gathered together at Charleston Farm, so visits – which need to be booked in advance – afford an opportunity to share the atmosphere of a historic and eccentric English lifestyle.

A bust of a young woman (above) contrasts starkly with the flint and brick garden wall. The spartan bathroom (left) contains a voluptuous nude painted on the bath.

Facing page top: a burst of colours and textures in a corner of one room, where a pair of ears, moulded on a plaque, hang alongside a rural painting. Facing page bottom: a marble statue 'cushioned' by a box hedge.

The first floor library (above)
is lined with bookcases
decorated by Duncan Grant
and window murals. Right: a
still life of a classical stone
head and a glassful of flowers
in the library, and (below) a
mosaic of stained glass set in
a door panel.

Top: faded yellow work files in a decorated cupboard and (above) well-thumbed volumes of Molière, Goethe and Marcel Ayme, all reminders of the literary interests of the group. Primulas, euphorbia and geraniums in ceramic and pottery bowls (right) in Clive Bell's study epitomize the freedom of colour and expression found throughout Charleston.

Mood in a Knightsbridge Basement

---◆---

Mimi O'Connell is one of the swiftest designers in London. She has an obsession with buying, decorating and then moving on as soon as her latest creation is a functioning home, planned down to the smallest detail. There is always an overall mood maintained in her style of decorating, of which this once-boring basement flat in Knightsbridge is a fine example. It has been transformed with trompe l'oeil paintwork, an irreverent mixing of antique and modern and the extravagant use of simple fabrics to make an elegant apartment that bears witness to the validity of a single-minded approach and an exact attention to detail.

Mimi O'Connell eschews any property which needs major changes to the basics, such as heating and plumbing, as these would take too much of her time. She has an incisive solution to decorating spaces and always works from available materials. Not for her the lengthy pondering over schemes and then the trauma of waiting for manufacturers' deliveries. She is also not interested in re-creating historical style, but instead uses her taste and the practical experience of living in her personally created environments to perfect her ideas.

The carpentry alterations and additional plumbing in this basement flat in Knightsbridge took only a month, and the decorative scheme followed with the same efficient organisation. Mimi O'Connell always gathers together the same team of builders as they now know her

Left: a basket of orchids in the studio (previous pages left). Previous pages right: the exterior of the Knightsbridge flat. Mimi O'Connell's style is refreshingly relaxed and elegant, as is clear in the dining room (below). Linen blinds (right) shield the internal window between the kitchen and the hall, which is painted to give the effect of marble panelling.

basic demands. Each room must be wired for sound, the lights must be controlled by dimmers and the telephones must have long cords – though, thanks to remote 'phones, this is now an obsolete requirement. Bathrooms must be white and furnished with over-generous baths. Nowhere are obtrusive fittings allowed to jar the decorative scheme.

The hallway of the flat was a boring space with minimal architectural detail, simply having two sash windows looking into the kitchen, and leading to a solid square staircase with no decorative merit. Mimi O'Connell's solution was to use the space as the background for a trompe l'oeil effect. She commissioned Chris Boulter to

make a relaxed and informal room in the round. Marbled panelling from the hall has been cleverly continued to conceal the heating panels. A red and cream design has been layered on top of 'Candido' beige and white striped cotton for the round table. Simple, white folding chairs from Conran have tie cushions in a matching fabric. This simplicity is mixed with an elaborate Regency gilt mirror above the bookcase between the hallway and the entrance to her office. The dining room, in contrast to the cool tones of grey, is in rich terracotta and red. It doubles as a guest room – a generous sofa bed and a table skirted to the ground in a red-striped cotton make the maximum use of the narrow space available. Massed tulips and white lilies complete the decorative scheme. One of the many views from this room comprises the whitewashed basement garden filled with white lilies, fatsia and rhododendrons set against a classical, nineteenth-century marble bust from Italy.

Mimi O'Connell's Italian background draws her to seek out exotic pieces of furniture. A favourite eighteenth-century Venetian bed is the starting point for the bedroom decoration, a fine example of her passion for using simple fabrics extravagantly. From a fabric-covered ceiling crown, she has draped yards of a blue and white floral print from Colefax and Fowler around the carved bedposts. The frequent use of wall mirrors cleverly increases the space dominated by the central bed. Painted borders in powder blue beneath the cornice and doorways also give visual scale to the bedroom.

The walls of the glass roofed studio – a half flight up from the rest of the flat – have been painted all over with a pale blue marbled effect to blend in with the sky visible through the rooflights. Trompe l'oeil doorways, windows and false cornices give architectural form to this vaulted space. To turn this into an elegant drawing room, Mimi O'Connell had a series of banquettes made to range round the room, and then covered them in luxurious Fortuny silk in shades of beige and piled upon them pillow-sized cushions. Four ceramic drums act as occasional tables, while at night the room is lit by low table lamps and a crystal chandelier found in South America. The carved gilt table comes from Nicholas Haslam and holds a collection of art books, plus large bowls of delicate pink orchids.

Thanks to her nomadic childhood, Mimi O'Connell regards change as a challenge. The idea of living in the

Blue and white floral print fabric hangs like a wimple from the ceiling crown over the Venetian bed (above).

rough plaster the walls with a hint of blue and then paint a dado of marbled panels in two tones of grey for the walls and window surrounds, thus creating a stimulating, three-dimensional effect for this space. The stair newel, balustrade and treads have all been marbled in dove grey. Using a basic stone-coloured carpet throughout, and having a large roof light placed over the short flight of stairs, gives a sense of space to what is essentially a narrow passageway. A functional, streamlined kitchen is shielded from the now elegant hallway by white linen blinds.

The irregular shape of the dining room – it has an open archway to the stairs, a doorway to the kitchen and a glass window to a garden area – allowed Mimi O'Connell to

same home for generations is anathema to her – she needs to change furnishings constantly, and to her this means moving on, as so often the initial style for a particular room, if right, is difficult to improve. Travel is one of her main stimuli and Italy her greatest source of inspiration, particularly in its neo-classical objects and furniture. Also she regularly visits the antique shops in London's Pimlico and New King's Road, searching for those affordable pieces with her inimitable visual flair for interior decoration. Indeed, much of the style of Mimi O'Connell's decorating is not seen, such as her antique, hand-drawn linen sheets – always pure white and changed daily – and her cupboards overflowing with snowy towels, but her everchanging arrangements of fresh flowers and greenery, which she never allows to grow sad, are a constant reminder of her dedication to detail – the hallmark of the Mimi O'Connell style.

Above: the short flight of stairs to the studio and (top) Mimi O'Connell in her study.

Above: a simple, elegant grouping of glass and cut lilies.

Mews House off Berkeley Square

Most owners settle for an overall theme in decorating – there are few who attempt to mix totally opposing moods in one building. This small mews house close to Berkeley Square in London has three distinct styles successfully executed in a limited space. No need to feel frustrated by city life with an escape route to country charm, an exotic study or a lofty eyrie for relaxation.

Mixing styles in decorating calls for confidence. Norma Quine is in the fashion business and her clear sense of style blends three moods in one small town house in the heart of Mayfair: Italian drama, Eastern exotic and rustic. The range could not be wider, and yet these elements have been successfully handled within the small space afforded by a double garage, plus one floor and a loft above in a cobbled mews not far from Berkeley Square.

With the help of architect Christopher Wilkinson, the house was sympathetically gutted leaving only bare brickwork and roof beams. A staircase and some small room partition walls were eliminated to gain every possible cubic foot of space, while the capacious garage was converted to provide a stark fashion studio for the owner's professional use, relegating the car to off-street parking.

The exercise in living style starts on the first floor, where an informal country kitchen atmosphere has been created in the wide kitchen/dining area that runs the width of the house. A variety of woods, such as old sanded floorboards, pine mixed with elm and reclaimed old pine doors, have been used to build kitchen cupboards, adding to the rustic feel, as does a sturdy butcher's block for a work table and various utensils hung

on meat hooks suspended from a metal canopy. Two fireplaces, uncovered when the building was stripped, allow for an open gas log fire at one side of the room and an Aga stove, set in a green-tiled recess, at the other. A handsome, eighteenth-century Danish gate-legged table accompanied by a miscellany of sturdy chairs make a relaxed circle for eating close by the fire, while white marble tops and green plants add to the rustic atmosphere – a totally believable one as a lovely view is

afforded from the kitchen/dining area now that a narrow
flat roof at the rear of the house has been transformed into
an attractive, white-walled garden. Here, plant-filled jar-
dinieres placed around the walls leave space for a table
and chairs.

In fact, space has been saved in as many ways as possible throughout the conversion – even a narrow gap between the brick chimney and the outside wall has not
been ignored. Although only two bottles wide, an expanded wine rack fitted vertically accommodates a dozen
bottles high.

A small study at the front of the house, graced with a
view of the mews, has been papered in mottled green,
increasing the jungle atmosphere that has been created
by the large palms and bamboo furniture. Lighting plays
a major role in setting the mood – hidden lamps cast
dappled shadows through the leaves. A serene, pale-
walled guest room alongside the study has the window as
the chief focal point. The bed is covered in deep blue
and above it hangs a cluster of Victorian fluted-glass
shades.

*Fire-engine red paintwork
(previous pages left) gives a
positive face to this mews
house. The bathroom's marble
surfaces (previous pages right)
contrast with its rich
mahogany woodwork and
verdant houseplants.*

*Above and right: a country-
style kitchen that provides
practical space for the
preparation and enjoyment of
food. A door on the right leads
to the walled roof garden.*

The gutted roof of this house makes a lofty, A-shaped space, reached by a twisting staircase that opens straight into the cleared area. Lit by a series of roof lights by day, by night it has been designed as a sanctuary to shut out the world: a haven in which to entertain friends. Black painted rafters make a sharply ribbed pattern against the white roof, setting the overall black/grey/white colour scheme. Dark antique furniture provides some strong shapes that serve to balance the black leather sofas, while the blank walls form a gallery-like background for a painting collection lit by spotlights hidden in the rafters.

The sleeping area of this chic residence is tucked into the gabled roof. As the roof is lower at this point it makes an intimate corner for the luxurious, fur-covered bed. The owner has again combined the 'window' (this time actually the loft door, which once would have been used to haul fodder into the loft for the stables below) and the bed as the focal point of the room. A richly beaded and fringed shade glows above the opulent bed, leaving the rest of the space in shadow.

The black and white loft sanctuary, with deep shadows and spotlights, contrasts strongly with the bathroom – a pool of mirrored light. Daylight, or the glow of the city at night, floods through the domed skylight to be reflected from the white marbled floor onto mirrored walls. Dark mahogany furniture, rich-toned towels and exuberant plants sharpen the style.

Throughout this terraced mews house there is a successful mixture of themes within the disparate rooms. Norma Quine believes in firm statements of style – and when a point is to be made, it is made boldly and positively.

Above: a fur-covered bed that nearly fills the width between the roof rafters. The scale changes (below) in the loft space to give the owner a private sanctuary.

Roof lights (facing page) and white walls provide a crisp exhibition space for an exciting collection of pictures. After these plain, strong tones, the study (right) is an abrupt swing to pattern, colour and shadows cast by spot lighting. The style changes in design to meet alterations of mood for a varied lifestyle.

FLOOR SPACE DESIGN BY BOB MCLAREN

◇

Bob McLaren, who converts run-down buildings as a pastime, has converted another Hampstead 'wreck' into an exciting open space. Two clear areas – one public, one private – both follow identical defined shapes and colours. The arched doorways and colonnades in the garden repeat in windows and bathroom shapes, and sharp yellow enlivens deep grey for this conversion of a derelict stable-cum-studio building.

The spacious, grey-tiled conservatory (facing page), designed as a tonal exercise in black and chrome, opens onto a patio garden. Brick colonnades (right) to the garden entrance link the arch shapes that are found throughout the house.

The building had both the right proportions and architectural integrity – Bob McLaren's basic criteria of high ceilings and big skylights – although much of it was covered with brickwork. It also had damp – rising, falling, vertical and horizontal – with a couple of patches of dry rot thrown in for good measure. However, it was not actually falling down.

In fact the old structure represented something like 225 square metres of potentially stunning space – a challenge that was absolutely irresistible to this intrepid designer. No records relating to the origin of the building exist, but judging from its location between two streets of late-Victorian houses in St John's Wood, it was clearly constructed much earlier, probably as a stable and coach-house for the gentry on nearby Hamilton Terrace. Converted into a studio early this century by the addition of big, north-facing skylights, it is known to have been used by the painter and graphic artist, Allison, whose idyllic, sunny posters for seaside resorts graced railway platforms and brightened the lives of passengers for almost thirty years.

First the building was stripped and repaired, and then the exercise in 'floor space' commenced. A former greenhouse project had clustered spaces together, while the objective of this exercise was to explode this cluster concept. By providing privacy with a judicious use of

The structural beauty of the Victorian metal trusses (above) are evident from the cantilevered bedroom, under which lies the mezzanine library-cum-music-TV area (below).

The 'public' living area (left) begins at the front door and leads through arched doorways into the conservatory. A spacious seating unit from Zanotta stands on an island of carpet, leaving wide, clear spaces of planked flooring.

The kitchen (below) follows McLaren's three edicts: function, form and fun. The first edict is fulfilled by a rigorous streamlining that incorporates an Aga cooker, work units and a tiled, island working surface. The table, chairs and lamp add the second, while yellow and white tiles add the fun element to this cool grey and white design.

room dividers and cantilevered balconies, there are big, open spaces without the hindrances of doors, the only two remaining being in the bathrooms.

The dominant pyramid form that had characterized his earlier work here gives way to the arch. Doorways, windows, bathroom and the brick colonnade in the garden all conform to this shape. In addition to abandoning pyramids, Bob McLaren also changes from the red palette he had worked on for two former exercises in favour of brilliant yellow, in which he paints the original Victorian steel trusses. Teamed with cool grey, it is also a motif in the vast kitchen and in both bathrooms, but his low-tech tendency has been modified, partly out of respect for the character of the building, and partly in favour of the 'clean-classicism' he employs to tread the delicate line between the last century and this.

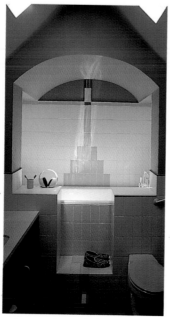

A bed, designed by David Field, dominates the balcony sleeping area (above). Lying on it, one can see the sky through a rooflight directly above. McLaren's yellow and white tribute to the bath (right) is his passing nod at post-modernism. This tiling exercise he designed as he went along, assisted by a brilliant tiler who cut and stuck as the design evolved.

'It's too easy to decorate and simply comply with the character of the building,' he says, 'and it's equally easy to do a contemporary number, but it's awfully difficult to dove-tail the two tastefully and live with the result.'

It is especially difficult when you need to house an unusual collection of furniture, paintings, books and esoteric paraphernalia. His collection spans the design decades of this century and ranges from a Twenties ticker-tape machine, through to a Thirties toy train, a Forties forerunner of the juke box, a Fifties turntable and a Sixties plastic E-Type Jaguar – a model of the one he drives.

'Floor space' consists of a public living area measuring roughly fifteen-by-six metres. A grey seating unit by Zanotta, a classic Arco lamp and a Marcuso table make one area, with an open dining/kitchen space coloured in grey and yellow. This space opens through

McLaren's desk in his work
area (left) is a Morozzi
'Tangram' table. This is
coupled with Magistretti's
Sinbad chairs, over which
hangs an abstract painting in
charcoal and midnight blue.
Light from the louvred roof
light highlights the graphic

The large conservatory (right) faithfully follows a dominant characteristic of the old stable, the arch. A brilliant joiner's sympathetic craftsmanship enabled McLaren to build this complex grey structure. The steel-grey tiled floor makes a sparse background for a prototype dining table by Rene Herbst, perfectly complimented by Gae Aulentis 'Solus' chairs.

Above: McLaren's clear work table and (right) the view of the adjoining gardens from the first floor. Chrome metal, grey paint and yucca trees (below) combine with a framework of arches to unify this building's design.

arched glass doors to the garden dining room in the conservatory.

The private living area on the first floor houses a formal arrangement of Magistretti 'Sinbad' chairs and a pair of Cubist-Deco tables by David Field, along with an original Rietveld red, blue and yellow chair, a chaise longue by Mattheson, a huge verandah chair by Magistretti and a cluster of Aalvaar Aalto pieces.

The mezzanine library/music centre is literally built-in to one end of the old building, the seating hiding extensive storage, and the wall of brilliant yellow shelving made by David Field being stuffed with books, magazines, quadraphonic hi-fi and a maxi TV monitor. McLaren says he is not a TV snob, but he is fascinated by the medium – which is just as well as, among other things, he writes TV commercials.

Frustrated house owners often ask how long these creations take. McLaren's answers simply 'Nine months from conception to delivery.' Though there are numerous indications of specific influences in his work, McLaren says 'I like to think that I have a totally objective attitude and open mind when it comes to sources of inspiration or influence. I abide by the doctrine that form follows function but, above all, I believe in the third F - fun.' And that is something all McLaren buildings exhibit.

LONDON COUNTRY RETREAT

◇

Canonbury House in London is a unique example of an eighteenth-century residence which has avoided the encroachment of alteration and development for the last two hundred years. Built as an elegant town house in 1770 in what were then quiet surroundings, the present owner has restored the architectural details of the period in a successful attempt to bring to the interior a tranquil atmosphere far removed from the pressures of twentieth-century life. As such, John Addey's home in central London is not a typical town house. Though just a few minutes drive from the City, it is graced with the calm of an elegant home – a 'weekend retreat' without the inevitable car trek to the country.

Having tired of the pendulum existence of a two-base life (an apartment close to Piccadilly and a country house in Brighton), John Addey resolved to merge his worlds. After a dedicated search he found an unloved Georgian house in Canonbury with a potential garden hidden under seasons of grimy leaves. Built in 1770, the structure's essential Georgian elegance had been blunted by some of its subsequent owners. Inconsistent Victorian and Edwardian additions were painstakingly removed and replaced with details true to eighteenth-century architecture. Ceilings in danger of collapse were replaced and cornice mouldings almost lost under decades of paint stripped down. Replicas were made from the original mould to unify the period statement in each room.

Perhaps the quintessence of a country home is a room full of filtered sunlight from the garden – difficult to simulate in a town house with only a small back garden. Undaunted, John Addey has trapped and reflected all the natural light available in his rooms by painting the ceilings in a high gloss, in Georgian style, while varnishing other surfaces to give a quiet sheen. Throughout, subtle variations in paint tones have been enhanced by varnish, dragging or marbling and all the colours fall into a warm spectrum of rusts and ochres, occasionally cooled by creams and deep blues.

The entrance is impressive. Double front doors open into a double-arched hallway lit by a pair of fanlights that are enhanced by delicate tracery. Soft ochre marble-painted walls, finished with varnish, reflect the pleasing proportions of the Georgian doorways and ceiling mouldings, while the doors, architraves and skirtings are drag painted in subtle greys with an undertone of green. A pair of grey marble obelisks complete the formal style.

The morning room, leading off the hallway, has the dado rail and the wall below marbled in pale brown to echo the marble fireplace. The walls above are drag painted in shades of soft apricot, while the intricate ceiling mouldings have been painstakingly picked out in cream, rust and brown. A pair of sofas upholstered in a quiet cane design hold a collection of dark, strongly patterned needlepoint cushions, and the underlying tones of brown in this room are repeated in the classically swathed Paisley-print curtains.

The drawing room occupies the full depth of the house, and is decorated in cream, russet and blue with co-ordinated fabrics. A careful grouping of furniture and ob-

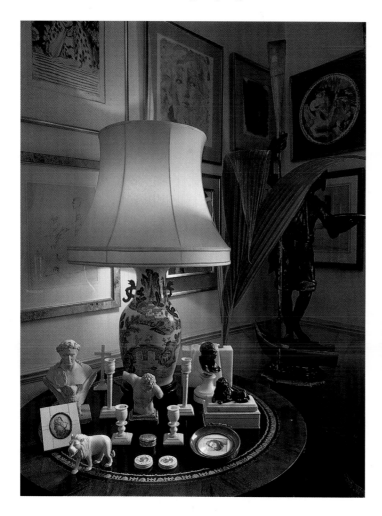

Previous page: the elegant exterior of Canonbury House. A leather-topped French Empire table (above) supports a collection of ivory and a Chinese lamp. The drawing room (right) occupies the full depth of the house.

Left: the walled garden, once lost under layers of dead leaves. With the help of the designer Peter Coats it has been transformed into a haven of green lawns and shady trees that centres upon a lily pond. Flowers planted informally provide a succession of quiet colour throughout the summer.

jects has reduced the considerable size of the room to intimate sections. A backgammon table has been set between one pair of windows, with two green leather chairs and modern navy blue sofas grouped alongside French Empire pieces and leather-topped tables. The varnish finish to the ceiling gives a mirror image of the daylight coming through the large sash windows, which have been curtained in a deep blue print. The fireplace in this long room has been painted to merge with the marbled walls so that it does not demand to be the focal point.

Eighteenth-century English furniture blends with classic French pieces to give a sense of quiet elegance to this house, while the rooms are bursting with paintings and objets d'art collected over the years by John Addey and meticulously grouped for his individual pleasure

Above: a marble-topped Regency table, graced with a pair of French ormolu candlesticks, two Georgian decanters, two silver-mounted tusks from Kenya and an elegant, Sheffield-plate biscuit box. The dining room (left) is designed to glow at night. Tortoiseshell vinyl covers the walls, and the brown ceiling is coated with varnish. High-backed chairs are upholstered in a fabric, which is designed to follow the carpet pattern, and is used again for louvre window blinds.

rather than according to the constraints of a collective style. Also individually designed by the owner, carpets with border surrounds have been tailored to fit all the rooms and provide a constant flow of pattern throughout the house.

The master bedroom is an understatement of elegance in navy, cream and rust, but the adjoining bathroom is opulent. The bath and basin are set in a huge slab of rust-coloured marble and boast Victorian brass taps, while the entire design is reflected by mirror-covered walls. By comparison, the guest bedroom, decorated with lattice wallpaper in yellow, grey and white, is a veritable sunburst of colour. The ornately carved white bed with cane wicker ends is covered with antique crochet work.

Flamboyant modern paintings lead down the staircase to the back hall. The pictures have been hung against slate grey walls edged by marbled grey skirtings and grey

A bow-fronted chest (facing page top) stands in an arched recess of the lower hallway, where the walls are covered in textured slate grey. Restrained elegance is the key in the master bedroom (facing page bottom), where navy, cream and rust, predominate. A black and white 'graph' design carpet leads into the adjoining bathroom (right), where the bath and basin are set into a large slab of chestnut brown marble. Varnish gives a welcoming glow to the marbled cream walls of the hallway (below), set with a pair of marble obelisks. The bordered carpets were designed by the owner and tailor-made to fit each of the rooms.

drag-painted doors, but these plain walls soften to a stencilled pattern of faded blue and red flowers around the garden door.

The basement dining room is co-ordinated throughout. High-backed chairs are upholstered in a fabric that repeats the carpet design, which is itself linked to that of the louvre blinds. The sheen from the tortoiseshell vinyl-covered walls is particularly effective when dining at night, and forms a rich background for a display of eighteenth-century French ormolu candlesticks and Georgian decanters upon a marble-topped Regency table.

Modern paintings and posters create a visual surprise for the visitor reaching the attic floor at the top of the house. The loft has been converted into a vast games room which, bursting with vibrant primary colours, stimulates a sense of release from city life. A vibrant blue pool table sets the mood for this room, which enjoys a bird's-eye view over London. Deep sofas upholstered in a modern, diagonally striped fabric invite one to relax, watch

An elaborately carved hall table and gilt mirror face the stairs (right) leading down to the dining room. Strong modern paintings on slate grey walls make firm colour statements here, while gentler stencil treatment of faded blues and reds surround the garden door.

television, listen to music or sharpen one's wits at the backgammon table to hand, while the skylight offers a view of the busy streets for those who just want to daydream.

Indeed, the whole house invites elegant relaxation, from the glossy entrance hall with its marble obelisks, through to the morning and drawing rooms, overfilled with cushioned sofas and chairs, down to the rich glow of the basement dining room designed for evening gatherings and, finally, out through the back hall onto cool lawns around a lily pond. When John Addey purchased Canonbury House its walled garden was lost under layers of dead leaves. With the help of designer Peter Coats it is now transformed into a haven of green lawns and shady trees with a formal lily pond as its centrepiece. Flowers planted informally give a rotation of quiet colour, splashed with white through the summer, while evergreen shrubs and creepers keep the garden 'alive' through the winter. It is clear here, as it is everywhere else, that in meticulously restoring the original style of this eighteenth-century town house, the owner has also created the perfect retreat for a country weekend in the heart of London.

Treated in plain, vibrant colours, the vast games room in the loft (right), exudes a spirit of joy. Sofas are arranged for conversation or solitary reading, while the games table and a pool table invite relaxation. Modern paintings and posters (below) give a visual jolt in the attic.

EARLY-EIGHTEENTH-CENTURY MANOR HOUSE

The Manor House at Itteringham has a marvellously creative family atmosphere. Here, the art of marbling and line painting furniture and floors, although executed here by experts, shows how the sensitive use of colour and paint techniques can restore buildings and furniture at very little cost. Talent and patience can make perfect.

The Manor House at Itteringham is part of the vast Blickling Hall Estate in north Norfolk, once owned by Sir Thomas Boleyn, the father of Henry VIII's queen. Now administered by the National Trust, romantic Blickling Hall and its grounds are open to the public, while the Trust also manages over one hundred cottages and about ten farms, all quixotically numbered in sequence (rather than by street) from a map in the Estate Office. It must make a nightmare round for any new postman delivering the mail!

John Sutcliffe was the National Trust representative for historic East Anglian buildings for a number of years, and there is little, whether it be a building or its contents, that is beyond reach of his restorative skills. He leased the Manor House at Itteringham some years ago from the Trust, and started on the task of turning it into a home for his family. The Manor House, surrounded by six acres, had been occupied by tenant farmers for a couple of generations. Being more concerned with the land, they

The date of this building (facing page) is recorded in the keystones of the first floor windows, each being inscribed with a single figure

1 7 0 7. Above: the drawing room, a tribute to John's restorative talent. All the furniture has been painted and upholstered by him.

had painted all the woodwork dark brown and covered the walls with a miscellany of papers and lime washes. John Sutcliffe, with the help of his wife Gabrielle, has succeeded in rolling back this gloom by two rooms a year, which he squeezed in between his restorative work for the National Trust, his decorating projects for clients and his work designing book jackets for a select list of authors.

This house of red Norfolk brick was built in 1707 for the village blacksmith, Thomas Robins, who married into money. The stone over the front door commemorates this marriage with the initials T M R, and the date of the building is recorded by the keystones over four of the first-floor windows – each is inscribed with a single number so that together they read 1707. Thomas Robins' own craft can still be seen today in the curled latches on the original leaded windows.

The house has a classically symmetrical facade, as well as a rambling assortment of attics and rooms in a right-angled wing beyond. Once through the front door, you enter a large tiled hall leading to the sitting room on one side and the dining room on the other. The latter, which possesses its original wall panelling, was painted and marbled by John in a short week while Gabrielle was in hospital, as a welcome home for her to one more finished room. The round 'marble' table, on closer inspection, turns out to be wallpaper skilfully cut to make a pattern

of inlay, stuck down on a wooden table and then heavily varnished by Holman Sutcliffe, John's father. It was Holman who fostered John Sutcliffe's interest in restoration and design, as his pastime was restoring and decorating the family home.

One of Holman Sutcliffe's gifts to his young son was an eighteenth-century chair, purchased for £1. This probably started off his child's appreciation of furniture and what began as a father's pastime has been taken up as a career by his son. He has, in fact, had his childhood present copied by local craftsmen to make an impressive set of six rush-seated chairs for the dining room at Itteringham Manor. Painted by the Sutcliffes in soft red and lined with grey to pick out the original design, their elegance belies their cost of £7 each.

Picture frames painted to match the chairs show the individual pages of a calendar commissioned by Wiggins Teape from Rex Whistler. The fireplace in this room, which also serves as Gabrielle's music room, is surrounded by 'Delft' tiles with a difference; each one has been painted by Gabrielle and John to represent their friends by their personal quirks, such as a cocktail glass for one, an airplane for another.

The drawing room across the hall has been turned into a very elegant room, its wooden floor painted to appear as if it were tiled with cream stone and black slate. The

Left: the bathroom, a generous room washed in coral pink. Above: a still life of a blue and grey painted chair with a jar of buttercups and euphorbia. Facing page: the stencilled bedroom, where the designs are based on folk art.

Sutcliffes claim that the patience and discipline of such painting (it is necessary to leave fine lines of bare wood as the gaps between imaginary tiles) is simple, once the art has been mastered. Using such line painting techniques, John has restored, decorated and upholstered all the furniture for the room, being content to treat the classic windows quietly with reefed cotton curtains, pelmetted in tones of brown.

The kitchen was in the process of being reclaimed when these photographs were taken. A big pew faces country chairs across a simple, scrubbed table. A painting of the exterior of the Manor House decorates the back of a yellow rocking chair, while a diminutive, rush-seated chair for their son, Tom, has been painted sage green and lined with russet. The room is intended to be a

hospitable gathering place for friends, amid the scent of herbs and country cooking.

Upstairs, Gabrielle has turned to folk art to decorate their bedroom, where the walls are buttermilk yellow with borders of simply stencilled flower patterns. John's son, Sebastian, assisted in painting the wooden floor in marble tiles of grey and amber, while John and Gabrielle worked together on a design for the mirror, using as a starting point one of the room borders John created for the National Trust. A metal bed with a canopy, found in a local junk shop, is hung with finely printed chintz and a simple cotton lining.

A closet connects the bedroom to the bathroom. When stripping off layers of wallpaper, John found that the bottom layer still showed signs of reddish brown marbling

A father's gift to his son – an eighteenth-century rush seated chair (facing page) – sparked a latent restorative talent, of which the marbled dining room is a good example.

Above and left: the art of line painting used to restore furniture and to decorate a wooden floor. Natural cotton curtains, pelmetted in tones of brown, drape the original windows, which boast Thomas Robins latches. The cheerful hue of a yellow chair in the kitchen (above right) is reminiscent of the buttercups that abound in May.

– a happy coincidence, as this was the effect he had had in mind for this area: some of this original marbling has been restored, but the remainder has been added by John. In a recess facing the clothes closet, an open obelisk has now been placed to provide unusual shelves for a few favourite Delft and Chinese plates.

The inspiration for the bathroom, one of the first rooms to be tackled, was sparked off by a rather special pair of curtains from a previous home. These are made from a fine Colefax and Fowler navy and white print lined in coral pink – when drawn, the light filtering through them casts a soft, warm glow. It is this gentle pink colour that the Sutcliffes have used for the walls and the open cupboard that displays a collection of soaps and china. At this time a blue porcelain basin and loo (found in the local junk shop) was awaiting installation.

Numerous attics and workrooms lead off from the bathroom, all awaiting attention. Old houses such as this rarely divulge their secrets, though here the previous generations are felt in the atmosphere of the worn treads in the doorways and the blacksmith's original window catches from two hundred and fifty years ago, slightly varied by Thomas Robins from room to room. One secret was found by the Sutcliffes. When re-wiring the bedroom, the wide planked floor was lifted and a pair of squirrel skeletons were found, one large, one small, which were possibly a child's pets that were hidden or had escaped beneath the floor. In another room, a draughty hole had been stuffed with a fine kid glove.

This labyrinth of rooms finally leads back to the central hall and its wide wooden staircase, cantilevered from the wall. This has a curled dog gate at the foot, and part of a carved story of the chase on the end of each stair tread. The horses, huntsmen and hounds ascend until finally, on the top tread, one finds the hunted hare. This can only just be seen under its gloomy covering of brown paint, as it awaits John's intended transformation of it to ash white. Having seen how his genius with the brush can transform plain wooden floors and simple chairs, the stairs with the staggered hunting scene will no doubt be a story on its own, to be told another time.

ACKNOWLEDGEMENT
The author and publishers wish to thank all the owners and
designers of the houses that appear in this book, as well as *Ideal
Home, Hauser, Homes & Gardens,* and *The World of Interiors,* in
whose magazines these features photographed by Michael Boys
were first published.